Pinay (

*The Unsung Heroics of Filipina Resistance Fighters
During the Pacific War*

Pacific Atrocities Education

Pinay Guerrilleras

The Unsung Heroics of Filipina Resistance Fighters During the Pacific War

Stacey Anne Baterina Salinas

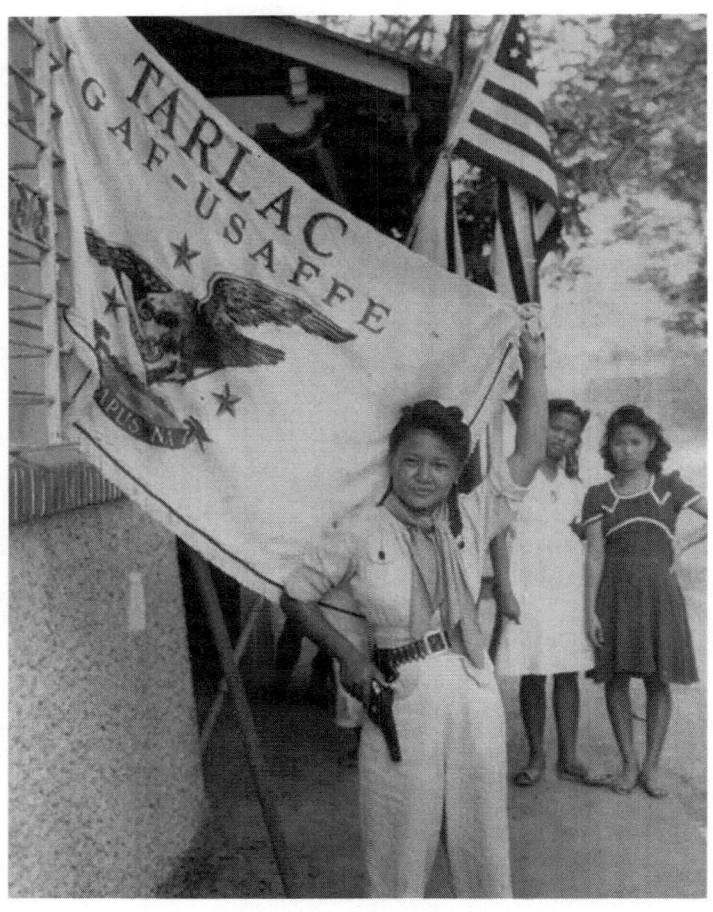

1945: 22-year-old Filipina guerrilla who fought in the Tarlac area of Luzon, poses with her gun, her cartridge belt and the Tarlac flag.

Pinay Guerrilleras
The Unsung Heroics of Filipina Resistance Fighters During the Pacific War

Written by
Stacey Anne Baterina Salinas

Researchers
Jack Gray
Jack Demlow

Editors
Nicholas A. Garcia
Jenny Chan

Copy Editor
Martin Mayhew

Second Edition

Published by Pacific Atrocities Education

Copyright © 2019-2023 by Stacey Anne Baterina Salinas
All rights reserved. Printed in the United States of America.
No part of this book may be reproduced in any manner whatsoever without written permission except in the case of brief quotations embodied in critical articles and reviews. For more information, contact Pacific Atrocities Education, 1693 Polk Street #1070, San Francisco, CA 94109

Paperback ISBN: 978-1-947766-50-1
E-book ISBN: 978-1-947766-49-5

Table of Contents

Acknowledgments ix
About the Author xiii
Notes about the Terminology xiv

Introduction 1

Chapter 1. The Japanese Occupation of the Philippine Islands: Pinays Answering the Call to Arms 11
Absence of the Filipina Resistance Fighter: Filling the Gaps of Women's World History 28

Chapter 2. The Hearts of the Huk: The Fierce *Heneralas* and *Kumanders* of the Hukbalahap Guerrillas 37
Felipa Culala of Candaba, Kumander Dayang-Dayang 42
Kumander Guerrero, Simeona Punsalan-Tapang of San Simon 46
Comfort Woman: Maria Rosa Henson 52

Chapter 3. The Glamorous *Guerrilleras:* Amazons of the Pacific Theater 61
Colonel Yay Panlilio 65
Kumander Liwayway, a.k.a. Remedios Gomez 78
Josefa Borromeo Capistrano 80
Nieves Fernandez 84

Chapter 4. Filipina American Veterans: Recovering the Extraordinary Feats of the Ordinary Pinays   **91**
  Josefina Veluya-Guerrero   93
  Corporal Magdalena Leones   97
  Lourdes Poblete   102
  Serapia Estojero Aremas   113
  Lourdes Evangelista-Castro   122

Chapter 5. The Legacy of the Asian Woman Soldier   **129**
  Public Memory and Remembering the Filipina War Hero   130

Conclusion   **145**

Works Cited   **155**

Acknowledgments

Writing a history about extraordinary heroines is no ordinary feat. Researching women's wartime experiences and contributions is unmistakably a tall order. Thoroughly covering Filipina guerrilla history required knowledge of the historiographies of various fields, including World War II, women's, American, Asian American, immigration, Philippines', transnational, and Pacific history. As a scholar of Asian American and American women's history, I had to capture the multifaceted vastness of knowledge this book required in order to do justice to the heroes of the Pacific Theater. Such a task required the time and energy of other patient and helpful hands. I would like to thank Jack Gray and Jack Demlow for their correspondence, research, and brilliant notes on MacArthur's Pacific Campaign. To fellow *pinay* historian, Abby Gayle Principe, I offer my many thanks as she was kind enough to contribute to this project by interviewing her family elders who witnessed the war first-hand. I am grateful for Pacific Atrocities Education's (PAE) know-how, and keen instincts in assigning me such a great team to accomplish this work.

On that note, I would like to thank the co-founder of PAE, Jenny Chan, for allowing me to continue my research and explore my passion for Filipino American women's history. Being able to find such a supportive, inviting, and warm institution of scholars, educators, and activists has been such a blessing these past years. As well, I would like to acknowledge Nicholas Garcia, who spent hours diligently line-editing my sometimes jumbled words, which I personally would not have been able to find time for as I juggled graduate school, work, and everything in between. Thank you for helping me to find my voice from the various outlines, drafts, and lagging Google documents that this piece eventually transformed from.

Of course, I would also like to humbly acknowledge those who encouraged me behind the scenes during my writing and researching process. To my dear friends from the Bulosan Center for Filipino Studies, thank you for your love and support. To my peers, colleagues, and wonderful students from the Asian American Studies department at UC Davis; you all are a blessing. I also would not have the ability, determination, or mental toughness to pursue such a strenuous academic endeavor without the support of my family and mentors. This work, the culmination of those endless nights surrounded by books and computer screens, exists because of my family, who instilled in me my cultural heritage, and because of my mentors, James Papp, Kyu H. Kim, Robyn Rodriguez, Richard Kim, Kathleen Cairns, and Wendy Ho who told me to keep on trekking.

Acknowledgments

I would also like to thank the Aremas, Poblete, Magallanes, Albarico, Orpilla, and Dawang families, who were kind enough to share with me their painful experiences of the war. Listening to their first-hand accounts, being able to ask questions, and reliving with them as to how the war transformed their lives, allowed me the rare chance to step back in time and recover our peoples' histories. This work ultimately aims to honor the women whose lives and sacrifices dot the pages of this book. For without their tireless dedication to country, family, and freedom, the world would not know of the honor and strength attached to the meaning of being Filipina.

About the Author

Stacey Anne Baterina Salinas received her PhD. in Cultural Studies from the University of California, Davis. Her research focus is Asian American History, centering on the experiences of Asian American women in twentieth-century America's Civil Rights Movement(s) and their roles as leaders and organizers in their communities. She dedicates her late nights of research and writing to the many men and women who fought for her grandparents' and parents' native homes in the Philippines. Her maternal grandfather served as a Filipino USAFFE soldier, drafted from Baguio City, and survived the Bataan Death March. His history, along with her paternal grandmother's late-night tales of her terrifying confrontations with Japanese soldiers as a young girl in the northern provinces of Luzon informed Stacey at a young age about the atrocities of war and the legacies it leaves on our ancestors and elders. Their stories and perseverance helped fuel her desire to write histories about the humble heroes and innocents who were unable to give voice to their struggles, wisdom, and experiences.

Notes about the Terminology

"Comfort Woman": A woman and/or female child who was abducted, sold or trafficked as a sex slave for the Imperial Japanese military throughout the duration of Japan's imperialist takeover of the Greater Pacific.

Fil-Am: Shorthand for anything or anyone that is associated with the Filipina/o/x American community, culture, or heritage.

Guerrillera/guerilyera: A female guerrilla fighter whose goals fall in line with gaining sovereignty or social and political self-governance. Guerrillas from a global and historical perspective often advocated for an end to imperialist, colonial, or state control through national, regional, or alternative forms of independence. Other guerrilla intentions included fighting for recognition as a self-governing party in a new state. Guerrillas tend to fight in smaller dispersed units and the soldiers come from all walks of life. The term's spelling can change and differ depending on the particular Spanish reference, the time period, or in other cases sometimes emphasizing the phonetic spelling.

Huk: The *Hukbalahap* was a rebellion also known as the People's Army Against the Japanese. The *Huks* were the guerrilla soldiers who made up the armed forces of the *Hukbalahap* under the main leadership of Luis Taruc. The majority of the *Huk* soldiers were from the peasant class and saw their role in thwarting Japanese imperialism as a way, if not a stepping stone, to secure democratic and socio-economic change for all Philippine peoples.

IJA: Imperial Japanese Army

Pinay: A term that highlights the working-class Filipina. More specifically, *pinay* is also a reference to a Filipina and her lived experience in the United States.

USAFFE: United States Armed Forces of the Far East

Introduction

The Philippines has a remarkable history of tenacious, ardent, and fiery female warriors. Filipino women, Filipinas, have demonstrated their cultural pride and admiration for their ancestral homeland through their military prowess and leadership. As early as the medieval period, Filipina warriors like Princess Urduja commanded armies, negotiated Pacific trade, managed tribal alliances, and shaped earlier notions of Philippine femininity and culture. Throughout her life, she regularly challenged the patriarchal gender norms practiced by her contemporary Southeast Asian rivals.

While traveling to Southeast Asia, the famous Muslim scholar and explorer Ibn Battuta recorded that the northern island of the Philippines—known previously as the land of Tawalisi prior to the era of Spanish colonialism—was single-handedly controlled by the multilingual warrior princess Urduja.[1] Her military prowess and skill at combat were remarkable. Confident in her abilities, Urduja proclaimed that she would only marry a man brave and skilled enough to defeat her in hand-to-hand

---

1. Davis Waines, *The Odyssey of Ibn Battuta: Uncommon Tales of a Medieval Adventurer,* New York: I.B. Tauris & Co, 2010, "Epilogue."

Artwork by artist Macabuhay depicting the Philippine medieval warrior princess Urduja, circa 1940.[2]

---

2. Ligaya, "Princess Urduja: Folk Hero's/Heroines from the Philippines," last modified 28th, 2012, last accessed August 24th, 2018, http://pinoy-culture.tumblr.com/post/26084878583/princess-urduja-folk-herosheroines-from-the.

combat.³ Her armies included both men and women. Her ministers and advising consul were comprised of female elders. She commanded military expeditions throughout the coast and provinces of Pangasinan on the island of Luzon. News of her military exploits and growing empire traveled as far as India, China, and Malaysia.⁴ Oral histories depict Urduja as the quintessential Filipina Amazon, and indeed, her martial victories continue to be passed down in traditional Philippine, Chinese, and Southeast Asian folklore.

There are other Filipinas as remarkable as Princess Urduja. These include the women who led and fought within major sects of guerrilla resistance against Spanish colonialism from the eighteenth to nineteenth centuries. One of the most famous and influential of these nationalist resistance leaders was Gabriela Silang (1723-1763). After Filipino Spanish loyalists killed her husband, Silang assumed control of his guerrilla units in Ilocos Sur. She is traditionally depicted as fighting alongside her countrymen on the front lines, leading the liberation of towns and barrios of the Ilocos region. Silang was more successful than her male nationalist contemporaries, leading colonial Spanish authorities to consider her the gravest threat to their occupation of the Philippines. The villagers and city folk of Northern Luzon even gave her the

---

3. Antonio Del Castillo y Tuazon, *Princess Urduja, Queen of the Orient Seas: Before and After her Time in the Political Orbit of the Shri-vi-ja-ya and the Madjapahit Maritime Empire: a Pre-Hispanic History of the Philippines*, University of Michigan, 1998, pp. 51-64.
4. Waines, ibid.

honorary title of *henerala*, meaning woman general.[5]

Silang was eventually captured and executed by the Spanish, but not before she dealt major blows to their infantry and confidence as a colonial empire. As such, even after her death, Silang would continue to hold an elevated position in Filipino oral histories and folklore. In both Philippine feminist and patriotic artwork, Silang is often depicted holding a traditional longsword, or bolo, while on horseback. Due to her fortitude and courage in battle, Silang is celebrated as a Philippine heroine, patriot, and proto-feminist, who planted the early seeds of colonial resistance and Philippine nationalism.

The centuries-long Spanish occupation of the Philippines bred other Filipino groups like Silang's, groups that aggressively advocated for Philippine independence. One of these early groups was the Katipunan. Formed in 1892, the Katipunan allowed for the recruitment of women into their ranks. The efforts of female combatants during this period of Philippine resistance have been mostly overlooked, with the focus being more on the women working behind the scenes in supporting roles (couriers, nurses, supportive wives, and homemakers who fed and housed the guerrilla troops). However, this is beginning to change. In more recent histories, narratives of Filipinas taking on crucial military roles for the Katipunan movement have surfaced.

Gregoria de Jesus, the wife of the founding member of the Katipunan, Andres Bonifacio, was the first female

---

5. Alicia Arrizon, *Queering Mestizaje: Transculturation and Performance*, Ann Arbor: University of Michigan Press, 2009, p. 137.

member of the Katipunan. Gregoria accompanied her husband to the male-dominated meetings of the Katipunan, and fought in the guerrilla army against the Spanish and Filipino loyalists under the name of Manuela Gonzaga.[6] As a *guerrillera*, Gregoria also served as the Katipunan's Custodian of Records, and was responsible for keeping the organization's documents and funds in order.[7] When captured by a rival sect of the Katipunan, Gregoria was tied to a tree, threatened with beatings by male soldiers, and robbed of her valuable possessions—including her wedding ring. She was then savagely raped by Colonel Agapito Bonzon.[8] Even so, Gregoria refused to divulge the whereabouts of Katipunan leaders and their funds.

As vice president of the female charter of the Katipunan, and as a soldier, Gregoria—like so many other unsung guerrilla heroes—advocated for Philippine nationalism and independence and thus was more than just a supporting character in the grander narrative of the Philippine Revolt.[9] And, above all else, because Gregoria

---

6. Robert H. Boyer, *Sundays in Manila,* Quezon City: The University of the Philippines Press, 2010, p. 136.
7. Ligaya Caballes, "10 Kickass Pilipina Warriors that You Probably Never Heard of," *Pinoy Culture.com: Your Source for Everything Pilipino*, last modified August 28th, 2014, last accessed August 23rd, 2018, http://pinoy-culture.com/10-kickass-pilipina-warriors-in-history-that-you-probably-never-heard-of/.
8. Cecilio D. Duka, *Struggle for Freedom,* Manila: Rex Publishing, 2008, pp. 150-152.
9. The Katipunan's "female charter" was essentially a female-run version of the larger organization. Historically, Filipino movements tend to work this way, with female factions splintering from male-led central organizations. While these female factions share essentially the same goals as

preserved the Katipunan's records, we not only know more about its mission and the nationalist rhetoric it employed, but we also have access to the legacies of Filipina wartime activism that otherwise would have been lost.[10]

Another Filipina guerrilla fighter, or *guerrillera*, whose valor serves as a testament to Southeast Asian women's political activism and military leadership during the colonial era, is Agueda Kahabagan. Agueda Kahabagan is the only Filipina to earn the title of general in the Army of the Philippine Republic.[11] Unfortunately, we know little of Agueda's life before and after the Philippine revolt. What we do know is that Agueda was appointed by the Philippine national hero, General Emilio Aguinaldo, to lead all-male units against both Spanish and American troops at the turn of the nineteenth century.[12] Like other Filipina Amazon-type warriors and *guerrilleras*, she is often depicted as a long-haired soldier on horseback, armed with a dagger and rifle. Known to wear white into battle, her compatriots gave her the nickname "Joan of Arc of the Tagalogs."[13]

---

their male counterparts, they often have their own unique identities. Florentine Rodao and Felice Noelle Rodriguez ed. *The Philippine Revolution of 1896: Ordinary Lives in Extraordinary Times,* Manila: Ateneo de Manila University Press, 2001, p. 17, 18.

10. National Centennial Commission, *Sulong Pilipina! Sulong Pilipinas!: A Compilation of Filipino Women Centennial Awardees,* National Centennial Commission, Women Sector, 1999, pp. 390-400.
11. Beatrice Celdran, "I Am… Woman: Historic Filipinas," *Philippine Tatler,* last modified August 7th, 2014, last accessed August 23rd, 2018, https://ph.asiatatler.com/life/i-am-woman.
12. Caballes, ibid.
13. D.J. Walker, *Spanish Women and the Colonial Wars,* Baton Rouge: Louisiana State University Press, May 2008, p. 13, 14.

Introduction

After the Spanish-American War, a new generation of *guerrilleras* continued the fight against American colonization. American propaganda claimed that they were in the Philippines to aid their "brown brothers" by teaching them democracy and nurturing their potential for self-determination.[14] In reality, the Americans merely sought to import cheap Philippine labor to fuel their growing agricultural industries in Hawaii and the American Pacific Northwest. To this end, American businesses exploited the islands' natural resources and their people. Furthermore, the American protectorate system continued to oversee and take advantage of Spain's colonial-semi-feudal land system, offering major seats of power to rich landowners, leaving most of the population at a bare subsistence level.[15]

In response to American and Philippine elites' mismanagement and profiteering during the early twentieth century, the Sakdalista Movement, founded by Benigno Ramos in 1930, advocated for immediate Philippine independence as well as estate redistribution. Salud Algabre, another Filipina *guerrillera*, directed several operations during the 1930s Sakdalista Movement, and was the only female Sakdalista military recruit to achieve the title of general.[16]

---

14. Kevin L. Nadal, *Filipino American Psychology: A Handbook of Theory, Research, and Clinical Practice,* Bloomington: Authorhouse, 2009, p. 94.
15. Peter A. Poole, *Politics and Society in Southeast Asia,* North Carolina: McFarland & Company, 2009, p. 159, 160.
16. John Witeck, "Introduction," as found in *Navigating Islands and Continents: Conversations and Contestations in and Around the Pacific, Selected Essays Vol. 17,* Honolulu: College of Languages, Linguistics and

The Japanese occupation of the Philippine Islands mirrored earlier efforts by Spain and the United States, in that they attempted to exact absolute control over Filipino culture, government, trade, labor, natural resources, and peoples. The liberation of the Philippines from the Japanese Imperial Army, like the past revolts against Spanish and American regimes, required the combined efforts of men and women from all walks of life. As with our previous examples, the efforts of the women who contributed to the war effort against the Japanese have largely been ignored. Indeed, Filipinas have either been highlighted for the supporting roles they played or more often than not, as helpless victims. The erasure of women's contributions to these resistance efforts perpetuates the notion that war, military, and state formation are territories exclusive to men. On the contrary, we have seen how women of color like Urduja, Agueda, and Gregoria served as soldiers and military leaders, demonstrating the extent to which the creation of an independent Philippine state required the participation of women to succeed.

The Philippine revolts at the turn of the nineteenth century—and well into the first half of the twentieth century—represent major stages where Filipinas demonstrated their nationalist and political fervor. The invasion of the Philippine Islands in January of 1942 served as yet another hurdle on the road toward Philippine independence. However, as with previous colonial invasions, Fil-

---

Literature University of Hawai'i and the East West Center, 2000, ed. Cynthia Franklin, Ruth Hsu, Suzanne Kosanke, p. 8.

ipina *guerrilleras* heeded the call to defend their lands from yet another oppressive imperial occupation.

Above all else, this book is a testament to the experiences, struggles, and contributions of the Filipina women who fought for Philippine independence in the Pacific Theater. Without their steadfastness, selflessness, and courage to protect their loved ones, home, and country, the liberation of the Philippines would have failed, and MacArthur, along with the rest of the United States Armed Forces of the Far East (USAFFE), would not have been able to regain their foothold in the Pacific.

Chapter 1

The Japanese Occupation of the Philippine Islands: Pinays Answering the Call to Arms

The invasion of the Philippines was the culmination of many years of Japanese expansion throughout the Pacific and greater East Asia. The Japanese sphere of influence extended over Korea, Formosa (Taiwan), Manchuria, and Inner Mongolia by the 1930s.[17] Their imperial expansion throughout East and Southeast Asia proved that its economy could support a military on par with even its western rivals' militaries. As Japan began encroaching upon Western colonial territories in the Pacific, American President Franklin Delano Roosevelt's concerns regarding Japan's expansive imperial presence in the Pacific grew.

On December 7th, 1941, tensions boiled over. Japan's attack on Pearl Harbor, coupled with their earlier invasions of East Asia, and entry into Southeast Asia in 1942, reflected their imperialist attempt to create a

---
17. Masato Kimura, Tosh Minohara ed. *Tumultuous Decade: Empire, Society, and Diplomacy in 1930s Japan,* Toronto: University of Toronto Press, 2013, p. 103, 130, 200, 252.

Pan-Asian state. For both the United States and Japan, the Philippines was a contentious space for these rivaling imperialist powers. Japan understood the value of the Philippines' ports and natural resources as a strategic advantage in expanding its imperial presence in Southeast Asia. Furthermore, by folding the Philippine archipelago into Japan's Pan-Asia model, the Imperial Japanese Army could eliminate western intrusions and major American military strongholds in the Pacific.

Prior to the attack on Pearl Harbor, the Commonwealth of the Philippines was largely shaped by American colonial interests and policies. The Jones Act of 1916 formed a Philippine legislature guided by a newly drafted constitution, establishing the basis for a transitional government overseen by American policymakers intent on supposedly establishing a foundation for Philippine democracy.[18] The trend of American hands politicking Philippine domestic policies and relations would ultimately translate in the following decades into the 1935 Tydings-McDuffie Act. This act defined the Philippines as en route to becoming a full-fledged democratic and sovereign state under "American benevolence and tutelage," which would be guaranteed total independence by 1945.[19] By 1941, however, the United States continued to retain significant control over the islands, especially with regard to its military, as well as

---

18. Neil A. Wynn, *Historical Dictionary from the Great War to the Great Depression*, Lanham: Scarecrow Press, 2014, p. 186.
19. Bill Ong Hing, *Making and Remaking Asian America Through Immigration Policy: 1850-1990*, Stanford: Stanford University Press, 1993, p. 35.

Chapter 1. The Japanese Occupation of the Philippine Islands

maintaining a strong naval presence throughout the main ports of the archipelago.

Japanese Military Strategy in the Pacific 1941-1942.[20]

For Imperial Japan, the invasion of the Philippines pushed them closer toward their goal of creating and leading a pan-Asian empire. It also allowed them to oust their Western rivals, who had, within the last decade, refused to conduct further trade with them via FDR's Export Control Act of 1940.[21] Such embargo acts, and

---

20. Louis Morton, *United States Army in World War II: The War in the Pacific, Strategy & Command: The First Two Years,* Office of the Chief of Military History, Department of the Army, 1962, p. 106.
21. The Export Control Act of 1940 was authorized by the President, in the interest of national defense, to prohibit or curtail the export of basic

the West's intervention in foreign relations concerning Japan's expansion and imperial gains in China, Korea, and Formosa (Taiwan), significantly curtailed Japan's aims of building an imperialist empire to rival both America and European nations. Due to the fact that they housed American military bases within close proximity to Japan, the Philippines was among the first priorities for invasion in the Pacific Theater. Immediately after the surrender of the Philippine Armed Forces, the Imperial Japanese Army committed the first of many atrocities that would characterize their wartime occupation of the Philippines.

The Bataan Death March, as it came to be called, resulted in the deaths of thousands of Filipinos and Americans. The march stretched to roughly a sixty-three-mile trek on foot.[22] Forced to walk without food or water, and under constant threat of torture or death, Filipino and American soldiers who survived the march would continue to experience brutality, slave labor, and starvation within Japanese-run prisoner of war camps. Other survivors were forced to work on "hell ships," where they were used as manual laborers for Imperial Japan's navy throughout the Pacific Theater. POW sailors who worked on the Japanese hell ships were often left vulnerable to

---

war materials. Under that act, licenses were refused for the export of aviation gasoline and most types of machine tools to Japan, beginning in August 1940. Erik J. Dahl, *Intelligence and Surprise Attack: Failure and Success from Pearl Harbor to 9/11 and Beyond*, Georgetown University Press, 2013, p. 43.

22. Robert Greenberger, *Snapshots in History: The Bataan Death March: World War II in the Pacific*, Mankato: Compass Point Books, 2009, p. 32.

Chapter 1. The Japanese Occupation of the Philippine Islands

attacks and in many cases were killed by their own country's navy out at sea.[23]

The Japanese occupation of the Philippines lasted for over two years. While the Allies reconvened and fought their way across the Pacific, the Philippine peoples began a ferocious underground resistance movement. Japanese brutality, combined with a lack of food and medical supplies, meant that the underground resistance required all available hands and voices to lend themselves to the cause of liberating the Philippines. Guerrilla fighters ambushed Japanese patrols, sabotaged weapon production efforts in local factories, and secretly gave information to U.S. forces via radio and off-the-coast meetings.[24] The resistance movement prevented the Imperial Japanese Army from establishing total control over the islands by disrupting their lines of communication, pushing back their forces into more open and vulnerable terrain, and pilfering their warehouses of ammunition and supplies.

However, such effective and stalwart guerrilla subterfuge was confronted by the Imperial Japanese Army's brutal treatment of guerrillas, guerrilla sympathizers, and local civilians. Testimonies and first-hand accounts of the Japanese occupation given during the War Crimes

---

23. Raymond Laymont-Brown, *Ships from Hell: Japanese War Crimes on the High Seas,* Stroud: Sutton Publishing, 2002. Tom Bennett, *World War II Wrecks of the Philippines: WWII Shipwrecks of the Philippines,* Happy Fish Publications, 2010, p. 27.
24. Travis Ingham, *Rendezvous by Submarine: The Story of Charles Parsons and the Guerrilla-Soldiers in the Philippines,* Los Angeles: The Bowsprit Press, 2018, p. 106.

Trials following the war are filled with stories of the pillage, rape, and murder of noncombatants of all ages.[25] Almira Albarico, who was six years old when the war broke out in Manila, recalled the brutal devastation of the Japanese invasion. Her family moved out of Manila during the thick of the occupation and into the province with hopes of avoiding Japanese raids.

Almira and her sister before the war, circa 1940-1941, courtesy of the Albarico-Garcia family.[26]

---

25. Timothy P. Maga, *Judgement at Tokyo: The Japanese War Crimes Trials*, Lexington: University of Press of Kentucky, 2001, p. xi, 67, 108.
26. Albarico-Garcia family, "Almira and her sister," photograph, 1940-1941, Albarico-Garcia Personal Family Collection.

Chapter 1. The Japanese Occupation of the Philippine Islands

The IJA was notorious for taking food and other resources from the cities and local farmers, leaving many towns and barrios to starve. Almira remembers how families would fight over rations because of the scarcity of food. Her most vivid memory of the war speaks of the violence of total warfare waged in the Philippines. While walking to school with her elder brother one day, they found that the town they regularly passed by had recently been attacked by Japanese officers. Almira, 75 years later after the war, could still recall the scene she and her brother witnessed with great sadness and apprehension.

"The town floor was covered in blood."[27]
—Almira Albarico

Almira's extended family, whom she had been staying with, would also be killed by the IJA, forcing her and her family to move to another town in order to find shelter. Innocent civilians, like those that Almira and her brother stumbled upon, were among the many casualties of IJA raids. In other cases, family homes were taken by force by the IJA and turned into housing or headquarters for the Japanese soldiers. Ofelia Galvez Orpilla, who was 10 years old when the war started, had her house taken by the IJA, forcing her and her family to go into hiding in the hills near San Fernando. For the rest of the

---

27. Almira Albarico Garcia, (World War II Philippines, Los Angeles, Manila Town, *Manang* Pre-1965 Generation), interviewed by Stacey Salinas, 2019.

war, they "slept outside" and had no choice but to collect and ration what they could for food. Ofelia remembers seeing American and Japanese planes in "dogfights" and recalled how the war became a terrifying part of their daily lives and routines.[28] When the war ended, Ofelia lost her father to malaria, leaving her and her siblings to be raised by her mother and aunt who had also taken on the responsibility of raising other war orphaned cousins.

The brutal Japanese campaign in the Philippines resulted in multiple forms of civilian casualties and tragedies like those described by Almira and Ofelia. Other times, civilians were killed or beaten if they were seen as sympathizers or associates of the Philippine underground resistance. Sometimes, small towns or local families were charged with housing guerrillas, which in turn led to mass killings, kidnap, or torture conducted by the IJA as they tried to root out the Philippine guerrillas.[29] Bienvenida Pedraza Dawang, who was a teenager when the war broke out, remembers that the Japanese officers would regularly patrol the towns and provinces looking for guerrillas. Bienvenida lived on the island of Samar, the third-largest island of the Philippines, and even there, the underground resistance had a great following.

> "There were guerrillas in Mindanao. When the guerrillas come [to Samar], we feed them and

---

28. Ofelia Galvez Orpilla, (World War II Philippines, Guerrillas, Vallejo *Manang* Pre-1965 Generation), interviewed by Stacey Salinas, 2020.
29. Toshiyuki Tanaka, *Hidden Horrors: Japanese War Crimes in World War II*, Westview Press, 1996, pp. 21-26, 32.

they would eat in evacuation places when they stayed in town. The mountains and hills were plenty in Samar [and] that is where the guerrillas stayed."[30]

—Bienvenida Pedraza Dawang

Bienvenida recalled how Filipinas were especially vulnerable to the Japanese occupiers, as "the women were taken in Manila [as sex slaves]."[31] Throughout the occupation of the Philippines, local women both in the provinces and towns were kidnapped and turned into sex laborers, forced to serve the imperial army as "comfort women."[32] Thus, Filipinas faced the combined threats of rape, kidnap, torture, and death for volunteering or working with the underground resistance. Nevertheless, *pinay guerrilleras* forged ahead despite these insurmountable odds.

Other *pinays* chose alternative ways to challenge the Japanese occupation, often aiding the local guerrillas and *guerrilleras*. Ofelia Magallanes, born in 1929, was one such *pinay*. She first heard of the Japanese invasion while walking to school. One of her classmates suddenly stopped her and told her that there was no school because the Japanese had attacked. At first, it was hard for her to comprehend the news. While in shock her

---

30. Bienvenida Pedraza Dawang, (World War II Philippines, Guerrillas, Sacramento and Stockton, *Manang* Pre-1965 Generation), interviewed by Stacey Salinas, 2019.
31. Ibid.
32. Margaret D. Stetz, Bonnie B. C. Oh ed., *Legacies of the Comfort Women of World War II,* New York: Routledge, 2015, p. 75.

classmates told her the best thing to do would be to run and hurry back home.

When the Japanese arrived in her town, Cavite City, they forced Ofelia and other local children to attend a camp dedicated to teaching Japanese culture and language. This was intended to serve as indoctrination, similar to the methods Imperial Japan had used in its other territories and protectorates like Taiwan and Korea.[33] Ofelia's father, Bernardino Magallanes, was forced to work at that camp as a cook, while her relatives were allowed to continue to work in their family's tailoring shop (Reynoso Tailoring Shop). Some of Ofelia's relatives were forced to tailor soldiers' uniforms in Manila and thus had to leave Cavite. These transactions ensured their survival and granted them protection from the IJA. Simultaneously (and unbeknownst to the Japanese army) Ofelia and her female relatives also assisted nearby guerrillas, working for and feeding them with what little food they had. Like Almira and Ofelia Galvez's families, during the war the Magallanes family also foraged and rationed what they could. For the entirety of the war, the Magallanes family subsisted on *kamote* (sweet potatoes) while rationing what little money Ofelia's father earned while serving as a cook for the Japanese officers. Despite

---

33. Japan's government, in its imperialist efforts to control and lead a pan-Asia co-prosperity sphere, wanted to implement Japanese culture and philosophies in the territories and regions they had invaded and taken, so as to promote Japanese culture and language as the dominant leading presence in their vision of their Asian empire. Shih-Shan Henry Tsai, *Maritime Taiwan: Historical Encounters with the East and the West,* Taylor and Francis, 2014, p. 151.

Chapter 1. The Japanese Occupation of the Philippine Islands

lacking resources and being constantly surveilled by the Japanese officers who hired their tailoring services, Ofelia and her relatives all managed to deceive the Japanese and assist the Filipino resistance for three years.

Ofelia recalled one harrowing instance that occurred while she was working with the guerrilla fighters. Some of the guerrillas and their sympathizers had been caught and were subsequently forced to line up next to a pit. One of them was Ofelia's friend. Japanese officers proceeded to decapitate each person. According to Ofelia, her friend's hair was so thick that the Japanese soldier's blade did not actually reach her neck. She proceeded to fall into the pit and feign her death. She then waited for nightfall to climb out of the pit undetected.

On the outskirts of Cavite, there were units of guerrilla fighters who were in hiding. Among the guerrillas in these makeshift hideouts were their wives. Ofelia's role included washing their clothes in the river, cooking for the guerrillas, usually dishes consisting of what little rice and pork they could find. Ofelia, who at the time was barely a teenager, would also assist the wives of the guerrillas as their midwife and nanny, watching over the children of the guerrillas. Ofelia remembers how in the midst of the war, with food resources scarce, and the Japanese officers all over Luzon, she was able to successfully deliver the twins of one of the guerrilla wives that she had grown close to named Marciana Tagle. To be able to keep the guerrilla resistance fed and clothed, all the while taking care of the needs of the women of

Ofelia after the war, Cavite City, circa late 1940s.
Courtesy of the Magallanes-Principe family.[34]

the guerrilla camp was no small feat. Such gendered labor helped not only to bolster the morale of the resistance fighters but also helped to maintain and grow the community networks that the underground resistance relied on.

Ofelia recalls how all the wives of the guerrilla fighters would stay in one house, "so when they hear that Japanese soldiers are coming, they all have to hide. They start running—no slippers—they just run away because of the

---

34. Ofelia Magallanes, "Ofelia after the War," photograph, late 1940s, Magallanes-Principe Family Collection.

soldiers."[35] Ofelia's extended family members and friends who served in the resistance, including Commander Castaneda, the commander of the guerrilla fighters of that region, served as her lifeline. It was Castaneda who requested Ofelia stay and support the guerrilla families outside of Cavite. She did so until the United States Armed Forces of the Far East came to liberate Cavite towards the end of 1944.

> "*Malapit na dumating yung mga Amerikano.*
> (The Americans are coming [to help].)"
> —Ofelia Magallanes

Ofelia's teenage years as a guerrilla supporter and confidante offer insight into the lesser-known history of the remarkable and critical roles Filipinas served in the liberation of the Philippines. Although not a *guerrillera* who bore arms herself, Ofelia Magallanes and her female relatives were among the many women and networks whose labor directly challenged Japanese imperialism in the Pacific. By working undercover to feed, house, and support the guerrilla resistance, they too contributed to the Filipinas' untold heroism during World War II. Filipinas like Ofelia and her relatives persisted in contributing to the resistance effort knowing very well that the consequence, if discovered, was death. Nevertheless, Filipinas who supported the guerrillas, like Ofelia and her family, continued to have hope and faith that the resis-

---

35. Ofelia Magallanes, (World War II, Luzon, Cavite City), interviewed by Abby Gayle Principe, 2021.

tance would survive and that their efforts would reach the American soldiers who would eventually help the Filipino cause. Narratives of *pinay* efforts to defy the Japanese occupation add to the Filipina wartime experience. Though Filipinas like Ofelia could be victims of total war and lose family and friends to the Japanese invasion, they nonetheless resisted and challenged their enemies head-on, choosing to protect their family and country by aiding the resistance effort despite the constant threat of death looming over them.[36]

Other instances of Filipina wartime resilience and bravery, although rarely recorded, can be found in various Philippine and Filipino-American newspapers and journals during and after the war. For instance, the American Journal of Nursing in 1945 provided a short tribute to Filipina nurses, Bruna R. Calvan and Carmen Lanot, and Filipina doctor, Guedelia M. Pablan. These Bataan medical professionals saw firsthand the grim and cruel treatment of both American and Filipino soldiers during the Death March. The three continued to stay in Bataan, even after the Japanese defeated MacArthur and secured the Philippines, in order to continue to heal and protect wounded civilians and soldiers in hiding. They did this despite the ongoing threat of Japanese military violence. After their hospital was burned down by Japanese troops, they moved to a convent to continue their work. That convent was also destroyed, causing the Filipina-led medical crew to make their own makeshift health

---

36. Ofelia Magallanes, (World War II, Luzon, Cavite City), interviewed by Abby Gayle Principe, 2018.

Chapter 1. The Japanese Occupation of the Philippine Islands

War Department, Public Relations Office
Bruna R. Calvan and Carmen Lanot (left and center) with Guedelio M. Pablan, M.D. (right) cared for Filipinos and Americans at Hermosa on Bataan throughout the occupation.

The Filipina-led medical unit of Bataan, circa 1945.[37]

center by nearby fishing ponds, where they continued to aid in the recovery of malaria-afflicted guerrilla troops by forging paperwork for more orders of quinine, which

---

37. A snippet of the Bataan medical unit captioned "Dr. Pablan and her staff after they had returned from the fish ponds to Hermosa where they reopened their hospital when the Americans arrived." Source: May 1945 issue of the *American Journal of Nursing*. "The 10 Most Incredible Filipina Warriors of World War II," *FilipiKnow.Net*, last modified December 5th, 2018, last accessed December 19th, 2018, https://filipiknow.net/filipina-heroes-of-wwii/.

they sent to afflicted soldiers in the mountain camps via *bangka* (small canoe-like boats) across Manila Bay.[38]

With barely enough food and rations to sustain their own well-being, Dr. Pablan and her small cohort of dedicated nurses survived the war and restored the health and stamina of the resistance. Their bravery and dedication to their profession and the Philippine peoples would be recognized after the war. Both Philippine and American nurses who stayed to heal the wounded and sick on Bataan were given the title of "The Angels of Bataan & Corregidor."[39]

The Bataan Angels made the best of a desperate situation. The Japanese occupation placed civilians in constant danger and deprived them of their basic rights and liberties. The IJA also made life difficult for anyone who, like the Angels, sympathized with the Allies, as Japanese officers were specifically tasked with stamping them out. This, combined with the lack of trained military hands to combat Imperial Japanese troops, made the contribution of women an essential addition and asset to the underground resistance.

---

38. Sergeant Karl Ritt, "Filipino Nurses on Bataan," *American Journal of Nursing*, Vol. 45 No. 5 (May 1945), pp. 346-347.
39. The Pre-Medical Society of the Ateneo, "Filipina Angels of Bataan," *The Pre-Medical Society of the Ateneo*, last modified April 9th, 2015, last accessed December 27th, 2018, https://www.facebook.com/the.pmsa/photos/a.146528742097296/810066542410176/.

Chapter 1. The Japanese Occupation of the Philippine Islands

A plaque made in honor of the Philippine and American nurses stationed at Bataan, which can be found at the General Wainwright and Nurses Memorial on Corregidor. Notice that the names of the Filipina nurses are not commemorated on this plaque.[40]

---

40. Karl Welteke, "Corregidor-Then and Now: 503rd PRCT Heritage Battalion, The Fall of the Philippines, Battle of Manila," *Corregidorproboards.com*, last modified August 3rd, 2015, last accessed December 22nd, 2018, http://corregidor.proboards.com/thread/1848/general-wainwright.

Absence of the Filipina Resistance Fighter: Filling the Gaps of Women's World History

War is a hyper-masculine arena that emphasizes the actions of men. Indeed, American World War II histories, in particular, tend to highlight the victories of valorous male soldiers abroad. Such wartime narratives idolize the distinguished generals who commanded them and memorialize the steadfast presidents who used noble democratic rhetoric to steer their countries towards world peace. As popular and mainstream historical narratives regarding the buildup of the Pacific War demonstrate, the main actors of the war typically referenced include MacArthur, Franklin D. Roosevelt, and Nimitz. They are discussed alongside a handful of influential military leaders of Asian descent—primarily high-ranking members of the Imperial Japanese Army —like Toyoda, Koga, and Yamamoto. What this means is that most other actors, despite the significance of their actions, are left out of the World War II narrative. This includes the women discussed in this book, who, unfortunately, have tended to fall between the cracks of history.

American women during both world wars are depicted as demonstrating their patriotism through supportive roles as humble sisters and homemakers. American women fulfilled these supportive roles by rallying for war bonds and food drives and rationing meals and canned goods in honor of troops abroad. One of America's most celebrated icons is that of the wartime female patriot: the hard-as-nails defense industry worker, Rosie the Riveter, brought to life most famously by the artwork of Norman Rockwell and J. Howard Miller.

In the United States, World War II provided the economic gateway for women to branch out of the domestic sphere and work for higher wages as clerks, secretaries, or other positions typically associated with women who labored outside of the home. Women of color especially were allowed other job opportunities that had not been available to them before the war because of segregation, which on more than one front (race, gender, and national origins), narrowed their abilities for socio-economic mobility. Filipina Americans and Filipina immigrants throughout the war used these new windows of opportunity to secure both a steady income for their families as well as supporting the war effort and radically changing how Filipinos in America and the Philippines were treated and seen.

Filipinas across the United States helped to raise funds and send aid for the war effort. Through organizations like the Red Cross and their local Filipino Women's Club chapters, Filipinas in the United States contributed financially to the war while also boosting the spirits of their local Fil-Am communities whose anxieties and concerns during the time were at an all-time high. Throughout the Depression leading up to the war, Filipinos in the United States were racially abused, labeled as "Malay," and thus because of their national origins and legally defined as non-white, were ineligible for citizenship. They were exploited for their labor as migrant farmworkers and cannery workers, earning less than 12 cents an hour, and were denied every opportunity to naturalize.[41] Filipinos in agrarian towns were harassed, regularly shot at, and even bombed out of the labor camps they were housed in. They were blamed for the economic slump and were seen as competition for unemployed white workers. With the Depression looming coupled with a war threatening the lives of their loved ones back in the Philippines, Fil-Am communities throughout the United States opted to support the war effort in hopes to be treated as both first-class citizens while also securing the well-being of their families and country across the Pacific.

Pinays in the United States thus took on multifaceted wartime positions on the domestic front, advocating for Filipino men to be allowed to register for the American Army, as they were previously denied to serve because they were seen as aliens ineligible for American citizenship under the Tydings McDuffie Act of 1934. *Pinays* like Fil-Am actress and journalist, Pacita Todtod, advocated and organized on a national scale for the Fil-Am community to be allowed to serve in the armed forces. After receiving her letter which ardently requested that Filipinos be allowed to serve regardless of their citizenship status, President Franklin D. Roosevelt revised and signed the Selective Service Act in January of 1942, allowing Filipinos to serve in the American military.[42]

---

41. Dawn Bohulano Mabalon, *Little Manila Is in the Heart: The Making of the Filipina/o American Community in Stockton, California,* Duke University Press, 2013, p. 72.
42. Cicero A. Estrella, "Filipinos had to Fight for the Right to Serve their Adopted Home," last modified May 5th, 2005, last accessed November

Chapter 1. The Japanese Occupation of the Philippine Islands

Other *pinays* living in San Francisco, Vallejo, and the greater Bay Area would also work at the shipyards and other wartime industries as a means to both serve their country and earn a living to support their families and communities.

Other Asian American women who did not work in the shipyards and smelting industries supported the war effort abroad as Red Cross nurses, pilots, entertainers for the troops, or even as spies working within pocket resistance movements in the Pacific or European fronts. *Pinays* like Yay Panlilio who went back to the Philippines to practice writing as a journalist became a *guerrillera* colonel during the war. More common American women histories associated with the resistance include Margaret Utinsky and Claire Philips, who provided supplies and intelligence to the surviving POWs of Bataan and local Filipino *guerrillas*.[43]

Filipinas challenged gender expectations under the duress of extreme wartime by taking on active military roles, proving that they too were exceptional patriots and fighters. While Filipino women in the occupied Philippines faced the constant threat of sexual harassment and torture by Japanese soldiers, they were less likely to be arrested as spies or guerillas, as these were roles that the Japanese typically associated with men. Such gendered assumptions allowed women more freedom

---

13th, 2021, https://www.sfgate.com/entertainment/article/Filipinos-had-to-fight-for-right-to-serve-their-2632699.php.

43. Theresa Kaminski, *Angels of the Underground: The American Women Who Resisted the Japanese in World War II,* New York: Oxford University Press, 2016, p. ix, 200, 401.

to travel between villages, without the overly heavy suspicions of Japanese soldiers, who expected subversive activity from the male rather than female civilians.[44] Traditional perceptions of war as a male dominated zone made women ideal operatives for a broad range of guerrilla activities. Women were excellent intelligence agents, as they could get far closer to enemy-occupied territory than male guerrillas. They also acted as liaisons between guerrilla camps and civilian villages, where they monitored the safety and communication lines of villages that supported the resistance.[45]

Celia Mariano Pomeroy was one such *guerrillera* whose liaison and courier work was central to the resistance. Among her other self-assigned *guerrillera* duties, Pomeroy inspired and instructed local villagers and guerrillas, showing them how to organize and network while simultaneously rallying villages with rhetoric emphasizing liberation and democracy. She later became the editor of a resistance newspaper, *Katubusan ng Bayan,* or *Redemption of the Nation*. She was also made the educational secretary of the central Luzon Bureau.[46] Pomeroy would come into frequent contact with the Japanese as

---

44. Vina A. Lanzona, *Amazons of the Huk Rebellion: Gender, Sex, and Revolution in the Philippines,* Madison: University of Wisconsin Press, 2009, p. 55.
45. Ibid., p. 60.
46. Jim Richardson, "Celia Mariano Pomeroy: Communist revolutionary who went on to teach in London primary schools," *Independent Minds*, last modified October 22nd, 2009, last accessed December 18th, 2018, https://www.independent.co.uk/news/obituaries/celia-mariano-pomeroy-communist-revolutionary-who-went-on-to-teach-in-london-primary-schools-1806786.html.

Chapter 1. The Japanese Occupation of the Philippine Islands

A short snippet in *The Philippines Mail* about the "lady guerrilla, Carmen Ligaya, who used the radio to provide intelligence information to the Filipino resistance, and liberation morale to both Filipino and American Allied soldiers, circa 1945.[47]

she traveled between villages. She survived numerous ambushes and attacks while under close Japanese surveillance and was deemed a priority target by Japanese

---

47. The Philippines Mail Staff Writer, "Miss Carmen Ligaya Effective On Radio Daily," *The Philippines Mail*, January 1945, Steinbeck Public Library, Salinas.

soldiers tasked with ferreting out Filipino guerrillas.[48] With her close relations and networking with local villagers, Pomeroy was able to remain safe and concealed on her missions from the IJA.

Female guerrillas like Pomeroy were crucial in spreading Allied propaganda and connecting other guerrilla units to USAFFE intelligence. The resistance's courier system thus was highly effective primarily because women guerrillas took advantage of Japan's underestimation of women's capabilities in the war. Using gendered expectations to their advantage, Filipina guerrillas feigned vulnerability to acquire a strategic edge, catching the Japanese off-guard. In so doing, Filipina guerrillas became invaluable assets on the frontline of the resistance effort, working tirelessly to maintain open communications, establish networks, boost morale, and ensure the overall security and safety of both the resistance movement and Philippine civilians.

Working as female operatives within the guerrilla resistance required both mental and physical toughness. *Pinay guerrilleras* navigated male-dominated military zones where women were expected to conform to culturally entrenched gender conventions. Indeed, not only did they have to deal with misogynistic male peers within the male-dominated Filipino resistance effort but they also had to risk their lives infiltrating the violent and unpredictable areas occupied by Japanese imperial authorities and their Filipino allies (known as the *makapili*). In these occupied regions, a unique brand of hyper-masculine

---

48. Lanzona, *Amazons of the Huk Rebellion*, pp. 148-153.

Chapter 1. The Japanese Occupation of the Philippine Islands

"machismo" reigned supreme, forcing some *pinay guerrilleras* to not act fully on their liberal patriotic inclinations, and instead, forced them to conform more toward traditional standards of Filipina femininity if they wished to participate in the resistance. Despite these gendered setbacks, *pinay guerrilleras* held their own and were crucial to building the foundation of the resistance through their efforts as fighters, spies, organizers, and medical personnel. Thus, *guerrilleras* formed their own standard of patriot, soldier, and woman—a standard that intricately blended traditional gender norms and challenged machismo perceptions of female agency.

Chapter 2

The Hearts of the Huk: The Fierce *Heneralas* and *Kumanders* of the Hukbalahap Guerrillas

The only surviving artistic rendition of the Huk *Kapampangan* commander, *Kumander Mameng* aka Elena Poblete, *Kumander Mameng* of Minalin. She led her own unit and fought on the front lines. Her legacy as a war hero can only be found in two surviving verified sources: one written by Moises Lopez, a foot soldier who served in Poblete's squadron, and the other by the famous Huk commander Simeona Punsalan, who kept accounts detailing her time with Kumander Mameng, whom she considered a friend.[49]

---

49. FilipiKnow.net, "The 10 Most Incredible Filipina Warriors of World War II," *FilipiKnow*, last modified 2018, last accessed December 17th, 2018, https://filipiknow.net/filipina-heroes-of-wwii/#2_Elena_Poblete. Photo Credit, Joseph Dado, the Juan D. Nepomuceno Center for Kapampangan Studies of Holy Angel University.

The underground resistance during the Japanese occupation was composed of various organizations and units. Although all branches sought to liberate the Philippine islands from Imperial Japan, not all guerrilla groups shared similar philosophies on war or postwar goals centered on rebuilding a democratic state void of neo-colonial influences. Of the 277 officially recognized guerrilla units, the Hukbalahap was one of the most politically aggressive and motivated in their efforts toward liberation.[50] The Huk guerrillas threaded their resistance efforts with their left-leaning socialist rhetoric centered on achieving true sovereignty for the Philippines. In addition to anti-colonial sentiments, Huk praxis aimed to oust the Spanish and American socio-economic policy that enforced a semi-feudal land distribution system where wealthy landowners held control over the production of the majority of the nation's lands and therefore solely held the rights to the production of natural resources and manufacturing of domestic products, all at the expense of landless peasants and farmers who tilled the land for little pay and board.

The Hukbalahap began as a socialist organization composed of a diverse cast of laborers and grassroots activists; peasant farmers, workers' unions, Communist Party members, and both urban and rural laborers. The founders and party members hailed from both the

---

50. Larry S. Schmidt, *American Involvement in the Filipino Resistance Movement on Mindanao During the Japanese Occupation, 1942-1945, Master of Military Art and Science Thesis*, U.S. Army Command and General Staff College, 1982, p. 2.

Chapter 2. The Hearts of the Huk

Socialist and Philippine Communist Party, and throughout the 1930s, before the Japanese occupation, served as active nationalists and revolutionaries who sought an independent Philippine state. The leader of the Philippines' first official communist organization, the Worker's Party, was Crisanto Evangelista.[51] It was not until after the Japanese capture and executions of Evangelista and his head deputy, Abad Santos, that Evangelista's communist and socialist guerrillas unified in calling themselves officially as the Hukbalahap in 1942.

The name of their resistance branch, Hukbalahap, translates to "people who are against the Japanese" or "the people's army against the Japanese," and resonated with local Filipino communities who experienced the abuse of the Japanese military presence.[52] Evangelista and his CPP guerrillas were depicted as bandits akin to Robin Hood, who helped the defenseless peasant folk by attacking Japanese military centers and redistributing the supplies they confiscated. The Huks were so successful in their raids and strategy that the Japanese gained very little control and terrain in most of Central Luzon, the main island of the Philippines.

The Huk rebellion against the Japanese was composed of two main branches, the guerrillas themselves,

---

51. Robert R. Smith, *The Hukbalahap Insurgency: Economic, Political and Military Factors*, Washington, D.C.: Office of the Chief of Military History, 1963, pp. 3-9.
52. Major Lawrence M. Greenberg, *Historical Analysis Series: THE HUKBALAHAP INSURRECTION, A Case Study of a Successful, Anti-Insurgency Operation in the Philippines, 1946-1955,* Washington D.C.: U.S. Government Printing Office, 1986, p. 14.

who lived in camps in the forest and carried out operations against Japanese troops, and the BUDC (Barrio United Defense Corps), who were resistance groups based in the villages.[53] The BUDC operated as support units to the guerrillas themselves. The BUDCs and their members would organize local support for the Huk rebellion, keep supplies and food out of Japanese hands and instead give them to the guerrillas, and perform all the functions of a local government. By involving locals and their respective barrio communities, and authorizing them control over their own resources, the Huks placed a great deal of trust and responsibility on their fellow countrymen to aid in the liberation movement.

The emphasis on laborers' rights, land redistribution, and the eventual creation of a more egalitarian state made the Huk movement popular among the peasant and working classes. Evangelista's political ideologies emphasized socialist and anti-colonial ideologies, which in turn allowed for a blurring of other traditional labor spheres. Thus, the Huk movement was open to women's labor and participation, which attracted many women to its cause.

Originally, the Huks only intended to recruit men into their organization. The first women who joined their ranks were family members of its male recruits. As the war progressed, more women—whose family members were involved with the Huk resistance—decided to join voluntarily.[54] Male recruits were usually trained as foot

---

53. Edward Geary Lansdale, *In the Midst of Wars: An American's Mission to Southeast Asia,* New York: Fordham University Press, 1991, p. 7.
54. Lanzona, ibid., pp. 40-43.

soldiers or officers. Women, on the other hand, were relegated to support roles, such as secretarial, propaganda, or medical-related fieldwork.[55] The vast majority of the Huk movement's female medical personnel worked as nurses. Filipinas treated overwhelming numbers of both local civilians and soldiers who suffered from malaria and injuries on the frontlines. Huk communist rhetoric, combined with the high demand for fighters, volunteers, and nurses, made the Huk resistance an opportune space for Filipinas to become directly involved with both spreading patriotic fervor and aiding rebel efforts throughout the duration of the war.

War gave Huk women the opportunity to take on important roles that once were deemed suitable only for men. Like most underground resistance militaries, the Huks were constantly short of resources, meaning they had to rely a great deal on Filipina labor to make up the difference. Large female support staff meant that more Filipino male guerrillas were available to serve in combat roles. Filipinas supported the underground resistance not only by providing medical care for male combatants, but, perhaps more importantly, by maintaining lines of communication and building networks of the barrio, village, and town support for the guerrilla cause.

Filipina Huks were tasked with winning over locals, convincing villagers and townspeople to defy the occupying Japanese troops, and, most importantly, to provide the basic necessities such as food, medical supplies, and temporary housing and shelter for the guerrillas.

---

55. Ibid., p. 52.

Therefore, the critical efforts of Huk women—who provided the means for collecting the essentials for the Resistance—reveal the crucial role that female laborers played. Without the dedicated women operating as nurses, support staff, educators, and community contacts, the Huk resistance would not have gained enough momentum, and thus, would not have been as strong of a threat to the Japanese occupation.

Felipa Culala of Candaba, Kumander Dayang-Dayang

Felipa Culala was a female Huk leader that exemplified both Huk socialist rhetoric and wartime-bred *pinay* empowerment. Culala was the only woman founder and elected member to the Military Committee of the Hukbalahap.[56] Culala's military rank afforded her the title of Kumander Dayang-Dayang, a name attributed to a famous Moro princess that translates to "a Princess of the First Degree."[57] The title "Dayang-Dayang" thus had a deeper historical background that further reinforced her leadership position among the Huks. Culala began fighting against the Japanese immediately after their invasion of the Philippines, long before the Hukbalahap began to

---

56. Vina A. Lanzona, "Capturing the Huk Amazons: Representing Woman Warriors in the Philippines, 1940s-1950s," *South East Asia Research*, Vol. 17 No. 2 (July 2009), p. 134, 135.
57. Unknown author, "Dayang-Dayang: A Princess of the First Degree," *Dayang-Dayang: Sulu Princess*, last modified 17th, 2009, last accessed December 21st, 2018, http://suluprincess.blogspot.com/.

Chapter 2. The Hearts of the Huk

Artist Dos Garcia's rendition of Commander Felipa Culala, aka Dayang-Dayang.[58]

organize themselves as a military branch. When the Huk rebellion began, she and the auxiliary troops she organized added a significant branch to the Huk movement, leading to Culala becoming one of the four co-founders of the Huk organization in 1942, after the execution of its first leader, Crisanto Evangelista.[59] She served as the only woman elected to the Hukbalahap Military Com-

---

58. FilipiKnow, "The 10 Most Incredible Filipina Warriors of World War II," ibid.
59. Alfred W. McCoy, ed., *An Anarchy of Families: State and Family in the Philippines,* Madison: The University of Wisconsin Press, 2009, pp. 62-65.

mittee, where she operated as the head of Huk guerrilla units situated in the East Pampanga District of Luzon.[60]

Culala was known for making do with what little resources and manpower she had—especially in the lesser-known Battle of Mandili. There, Culala staged an ambush to rescue her captured guerrilla soldiers from within the Japanese holding of the barrio of Mandili (Culala's hometown), and, with less than 140 men, was able to eliminate 40 Japanese officers and 68 police officers, pilfering the remaining Japanese resources from the battle for the Huk guerrillas.[61] Though Culala proved to be a great military leader and strategist, she experienced a great deal of scrutiny from her male Huk peers.

Accounts of those who worked with Felipa paint her in two radically different depictions: one as a strong leader who had a commanding presence, and another as an overbearing, haughty, conceited, and power-hungry woman who did not heed the Huk rules of conduct.[62] It would be the latter depiction that came to define (and plague) Culala's legacy. Eventually, Culala's behavior "became so disruptive" to the Huk movement that her comrades put her on trial, convicting her of both tyranny and stealing supplies from helpless barrios, resulting in her execution by firing squad for such

---

60. Tonette Orejas, "Last Living Woman Huk Leader Gets Pension," *Inquirer. Net*, last modified June 24th, 2014, last accessed August 4th, 2017, http://newsinfo.inquirer.net/613833/last-living-woman-huk-leader-gets-pension-back.
61. Leonard Davis, *Revolutionary Struggle in the Philippines,* New York: Palgrave Macmillan Press, 1989, p. 37.
62. Ibid.

unwanted "behavior."[63] The extravagant nature of her execution served to characterize Filipina *guerrilleras* as unstable women easily consumed by their own passions, and thus, detrimental to the resistance.

The draconian execution and the paucity of reliable primary sources depicting Culala's actual personality and actions have reinforced the notion that Culala impeded rather than helped Huk guerrilla operations.[64] However, after the war ended, Huk women argued that Culala was demonized because she was a threat to the power and influence of her male peers, especially the chief of the Huks, Luis Taruc. In their eyes, the party worked deliberately to find the means of proving Culala's inability to lead or have a significant role in the Huk resistance.[65] The discrepancies in Culala's narrative reveal how gender hierarchies and a patriarchal culture defined the Huk movement.

The difficulty in finding reliable resources about Culala, along with the surviving depictions of her "infamous" and "excessive" behavior that condemned her based on characteristics attributed directly to her gender, reveals the excessive barriers of discrimination that Filipina guerrillas faced. Even in organizations

---

63. Luis Taruc, *He Who Rides the Tiger*, Praeger, New York, 1967, p. 129.
64. Marc V., "14 Amazing Filipina Heroines You Don't Know But Should," *FilipiKnow.Net*, last modified October 7th, 2018, last accessed December 22nd, 2018, https://filipiknow.net/greatest-filipina-heroines/.
65. Cynthia G. Franklin, Ruth Hsu, & Suzanne Kosanke, ed., *Navigating Island and Continents: Conversations and Contestations in and Around the Pacific, Selected Essays, Vol. 17,* Honolulu: College of Languages, Linguistics and Literature, University of Hawai'i, 2000, p. 8.

that afforded women slightly more freedom and recognition, like the Huks, women like Culala—who held multiple privileges (wealth, *mestiza* caste) and demonstrated soldierly resilience—continued to be marginalized based on rigid gender conventions. Culala's gender ultimately prevented her from living long enough to witness the fruits of her labor—the liberation of the Philippines. Nonetheless, Culala remains the highest-ranked woman in the Huk resistance. As such, she should be remembered not only for her contributions to the underground resistance but also as a symbol of feminist Filipina empowerment.

Kumander Guerrero, Simeona Punsalan-Tapang of San Simon

Another example of exceptional Huk female leadership is Simeona Punsalan-Tapang. Punsalan's accomplishments on the battlefield earned her the title of *Kumander* Guerrero. She joined the Huk after learning that Japanese soldiers were notorious for kidnapping and raping Filipina women. To protect her fellow *pinays*, Punsalan spoke with Hukbalahap representatives in her village and joined their ranks.[66] Punsalan served in Hukbalahap Squadron No. 104 from November 1942 to December 1943, before being promoted to major in 1944 under the 1st Regiment, Second Battalion Staff, Regional Com-

---

66. Lanzona, *Amazons of the Huk Rebellion*, p. 156.

Chapter 2. The Hearts of the Huk

Commander Guerrero, a grassroots socialist *guerrillera* who advocated for peasants' and farmers' rights before, during and long after World War II. This photograph shows a captured Guerrero in the custody of the Philippine government in Bataan-Zambales, circa 1948, courtesy of Rizal Library, Ateneo de Manila University.[67]

mand No. 7.[68] As a political advisor and networking courier, Punsalan kept local villages informed of Japanese encroachment. She single-handedly secured the safety of local Filipinos and boosted their morale by regularly notifying them of victorious Huk raids that crippled Japanese storehouses and further entrenched the resistance.

---

67. This photograph shows a captured Guerrero in the custody of the Philippine government in Bataan-Zambales, circa 1948, courtesy of Rizal Library, Ateneo de Manila University.
68. GMA News, "Last Living Huk Commander Passes Away a Day Before Her 93rd Birthday," *GMA News Online*, last modified July 2, 2015, last accessed December 18th, 2018, https://www.gmanetwork.com/news/lifestyle/content/514518/last-living-huk-commander-passes-away-a-day-before-93rd-birthday/story/.

As a courier, informant, spy, commander, soldier, and Huk recruiter, Punsalan served as an example of how, given the right opportunities, *pinays* had the potential to play a crucial role in liberating the Philippines. Indeed, as a result of her actions, Punsalan's legend spread quickly throughout the Huk movement. She was especially known for her steely resolve on the battlefield, where she participated on the frontlines alongside her comrades. Supreme Chief of the Huks Luis Taruc once described Punsalan as "a big-bodied woman with a man's strength, fond of wearing men's clothes and adept at handling an automatic rifle."[69]

Unfortunately, Punsalan still faced gender discrimination, often in the form of male guerrillas refusing to listen to her orders. On such occasions, Punsalan drew on both her experience as a leader of a patriotic resistance movement and her intimidating six-foot figure to put uncooperative subordinates in their place.

> "My command on the front line was for us to [create] a V-formation but my second in command refused to follow my order. I pulled out my 37 cal. gun and pointed it at him. I said, 'Now you will have to follow my command. He did."[70]
>
> —Commander Punsalan

---

69. ABS CBN Staff Writer, "Last Hukbalahap Commander Dies, Age 92," *ABS CBN News*, last modified July 3rd 2015, last accessed December 22nd, 2018, https://news.abs-cbn.com/nation/regions/07/02/15/last-hukbalahap-commander-dies-age-92.
70. Interview. Tonette Orejas, "Woman Huk Commander's Wish: Care for Huk Vets," *Philippine Daily Inquirer*, last modified July 1st, 2014, last ac-

Despite the sexism *guerrilleras* faced, Punsalan's accomplishments and recruiting efforts did not go unnoticed, convincing other women—like Gloria Rivera—to join the guerrillas. Rivera, like Punsalan, feared that the Japanese would try to rape her and, in an effort to learn how to protect herself and her fellow *pinays*, joined the Huk rebellion. Rivera would also rise through the ranks and take command of her own squadron.[71]

Kumander Guerrero's heroism and commitment to the guerrillas would continue long after the war. Not all Filipino soldiers and guerrillas would be granted the appropriate recognition, veteran status, and benefits promised to its heroes, particularly those outlined in the Nationality Act of 1940. The Rescission Act of 1946 signed by President Truman made sure to deny veterans' benefits to the Filipino troops who served with the argument that the United States had already paid $200 million in cash to the Philippines after the war for their sacrifices. This promised lump sum of money was never given to the Philippine government and thus never received.[72] The influence of American foreign policy making would not end after the war. The postwar Philippines economy functioned at the beck and call of the United States who continued to manage the Philippines both by providing economic support and by manipu-

---

cessed December 18th, 2018, https://www.pressreader.com/philippines/philippine-daily-inquirer/20140701/281612418494661.

71. Lanzona, ibid., p. 158, 159.
72. Congressional Record, *United States of America: Congressional Record: Proceedings and Debates of the 111th Congress, First Session,* Washington: United States Government Printing Office, 2009, p. 16040.

The late Commander Guerrero, aka Simeona Punsalan, pictured here celebrating her 92nd birthday and speaking on behalf of the Huk veterans and advocating for their service benefits, July 2014.[73]

lating government seats in the new Philippine government. This caused tension between the new democratic republic of the Philippines and other political groups, like the Huk and other socialist-leaning parties.

---

73. Ligaya Caballes, "Simeona Punsalan Tapang, "Kumander Guerrero", the last living Huk Kumander and proud Kapampangan, dies at 92," *Pinoy-Culture.com: Your Source for Everything Pilipino*, last modified July 12th, 2015, last accessed December 18th, 2018, http://pinoy-culture.com/simeona-punsalan-tapang-kumander-guerrero-the-last-living-huk-kumander-and-proud-kapampangan-dies-at-92/.

Chapter 2. The Hearts of the Huk

After the war ended, Huk veterans began a legal battle against the Philippine government for compensation and recognition of their service. Unfortunately, it soon became clear that these Huk veterans would be unsuccessful. Indeed, because of their communist ties, Huk veterans were barred from participating in the newly formed Philippine government. This eventually forced them into hiding, where they would take up arms yet again as a guerrilla force, this time with the aim of liberating the neo-colonial Philippine state from American control and Filipino capitalist interests. The United States continued to manage the Philippines after the war, regularly intervening in its domestic politics for the sake of "democracy." As a result, Huk guerrillas went uncompensated. Even worse, because they were portrayed in such a negative light by the neo-colonial Philippine state, their efforts to liberate the Philippines during World War II became increasingly underappreciated.

Kumander Guerrero, despite the negative connotations attached to the communist rhetoric of the Hukbalahap, would fight for the recognition of and pensions for surviving members of the Huk forces who fought throughout World War II until her death in 2015 at the age of 93.[74] By 2014, Punsalan had helped over one hundred Huk veterans apply for pensions and correct their military documents and records. She used her thumb-

---

74. Tonette Orejas, "Last Woman Huk Leader Dies, Leaves Legacy of Dedication," *The Philippine Inquirer, Central Luzon*, last modified July 3rd, 2015, last accessed December 16th, 2018, http://newsinfo.inquirer.net/702422/last-woman-huk-leader-dies-leaves-legacy-of-dedication.

print as her signature to confirm her fellow Huks' roles in the resistance and drew from her vast reservoir of memories about the Huk guerrillas as binding evidence of the major contributions that she and other resistance fighters made in the fight against Japan's occupation of the Philippines.[75]

Comfort Woman: Maria Rosa Henson

The fear of rape that spurred women like Punsalan and Rivera to protect themselves and join the resistance was well-founded. Eyewitness accounts reveal how Japanese soldiers targeted Filipinas throughout the villages and barrios of the Philippines. Such accounts of women being molested, beaten, kidnapped, and even mutilated by Japanese soldiers reveal the sexual violence women and children were vulnerable to in times of total war. Under Japanese occupation, women throughout the Pacific were forced to become sex laborers for the Imperial Japanese Army. Near the end of the war, when surrender seemed imminent, the Imperial Japanese Army ordered all "comfort women" to be killed, and all documents and "comfort stations" that might speak to their existence destroyed.[76]

Scholars estimate that roughly 200,000 women across the Pacific Theater during the Pacific War were

---

75. Ibid.
76. Eileen Yujoo Kim, *Korean Comfort Women: Political and Personal History Intertwined,* Berkeley: University of California Press, 1997, pp. 43-45.

forced into the sex slavery system implemented by the Imperial Japanese Army.[77] Many of these women survived the war, but few lived to pass on their stories during the early 1990s when international news caught wind of attempts by Asian women's nonprofit organizations who began broadcasting survivors' testimonies.[78] To this day, leaders of Japan's government and foreign relations, including Prime Minister Shinzō Abe, refuse to fully acknowledge the brutalities and exploitation of Asian women by the Imperial Japanese Army.[79]

Traditionally, women are not seen as combatants; they are lumped into the category of casualties of war. Such terminology portrays Filipinas as silent, helpless, and nameless victims forced into the tumultuous violence born from war. Thus, *pinays* who were abused and victimized by Japanese male soldiers are depicted as unable to protect themselves, and unable to possess the strength needed to further the goals of the Philippine resistance. However, such women who were "casualties and victims of war," and experienced rape, torture, or were killed, were not powerless bodies. The *pinays* held

---

77. Yoshimi Yoshiaki, *Comfort Women: Sexual Slavery in the Japanese Military During World War II,* New York: Columbia University Press, 1995, p. 91.
78. Miki Y. Ishida, *Toward Peace: War Responsibility, Postwar Compensation, and Peace Movements and Education in Japan,* New York: iUniverse, Inc., 2005, p. 71.
79. Tomohiro Osaki, "Abe Rejects Seoul's New Call for Apology On 'Comfort Women' Issue," *Japan Times,* last modified January 12th, 2018, last accessed December 21st, 2018, https://www.japantimes.co.jp/news/2018/01/12/national/politics-diplomacy/abe-rejects-kangs-new-apology-call-comfort-women-issue/.

their own, exercising a kind of strength and agency that demonstrated their resistance, political defiance, and participation in the war effort.

Indeed, many of the Huk guerrillas were incredibly strong women who survived beatings, rape, and torture at the hands of Japanese soldiers. Maria Rosa Henson was only fourteen when the Japanese invaded the Philippines. According to Henson's autobiography, *Comfort Woman*, while she was gathering firewood near Fort Bonifacio, a group of Japanese soldiers seized her, upon which each took turns raping her.[80] She was later found by a local farmer who brought her to her family to heal and recover from the physical and psychological trauma of her encounter with the three Japanese soldiers.[81]

Maria and her mother eventually moved to the village Pampanga to escape the Imperial Japanese Army.[82] Pampanga had a sizable Hukbalahap presence, and Maria was soon recruited to serve as a message courier, whose tasks included gathering supplies from the local villagers to aid the resistance.[83] After several successful missions and close encounters with the Japanese, Maria was eventually arrested at a Japanese checkpoint and sent to a "comfort station," where she became a sex

---

80. Maria Rosa Henson, *Comfort Woman: A Filipina's Story of Prostitution and Slavery Under the Japanese Military*, New York: Rowman & Littlefield, 2017, p. 29.
81. Kathryn J. Atwood, *Women Heroes of World War II: The Pacific Theater, 15 Stories of Resistance, Rescue, Sabotage, and Survival*, Chicago: Chicago Review Press Incorporated, 2017, pp. 101-103.
82. Ibid., p. 101.
83. Ibid., p. 102.

slave, or comfort woman, for the Imperial Japanese Army stationed near Pampanga. Every day in captivity, Maria was raped by multiple Japanese soldiers, anywhere from ten to thirty men in one day, who savagely beat and cursed at her.[84]

While in the comfort station, Maria overheard Captain Tanaka and his officers making a plan to attack Pampanga, her mother's home barrio.[85] The next day she was able to whisper a warning to an old man outside the fence of her compound. In turn, he warned the villagers so they may escape. When the Japanese officers discovered what she had done, they tied Maria up and beat her senselessly.[86] Local guerillas later raided the comfort compound and freed Maria along with other comfort women and POWs.

After her rescue, Maria lived with her mother for the remainder of the war. Her mother, Julia, worked every day to help her daughter recover. Julia spoon fed her daughter and helped her to walk again. Due to the extreme extent to which Maria's experiences in the comfort station had taken on her physical and mental psyche, simple movements and daily activities became daunting, if not impossible, tasks for her.[87] She rarely left the house in fear of being recognized by Japanese officers. Maria would eventually physically recover, marry, and have children with another guerrilla by the name of Domingo.

---

84. Henson, *Comfort Woman*, pp. 37-59.
85. Ibid., p. 55.
86. Ibid., p. 59.
87. Ibid., p. 61.

However, after the Japanese occupation ended, the Huk rebellion would continue with the aims of ending monopolies on land redistribution, social inequality, and the continuing postcolonial American presence in Philippine affairs. Domingo would continue fighting alongside the Huk rebels, eventually leaving Maria and their children for both the Huk cause and another woman.[88]

Nearly fifty years passed before Maria would speak about her experiences during the war. In 1992, a radio program about World War II comfort women aired and caught Maria's attention. She came forward to tell her story, with the hopes that other Asian comfort women would no longer hide from the cultural shame produced by the violations their bodies had endured. Because many Asian cultures are centered on patriarchal values, many comfort women felt the need to hide their pasts, feeling immense shame, as former sex slaves. Testimonies from Korea, Taiwan, China, and the Philippines describe these women as having intense and lingering socio-cultural notions that the violations of their bodies translated to shame and dishonor that was detrimental to their and their family's reputations.[89] Maria's bravery, which gave her the ability to speak about her experiences and narrate her role in the war, reveals the many gendered-levels of wartime that are often glossed over. In doing so, Maria was not only able to serve her country and people by relaying the bravery and grit of wartime Filipinas, she also opened up the needed conversa-

---

88. Atwood, *Women Heroes of World War II*, p. 106, 107.
89. Yoshiaki, ibid., p. 195, 196.

tion as to how Asian women should not be confined to the traditional female mold of pure and reserved wives and obedient daughters as it hinders their own health, wellbeing, and future.

In 1993, Maria and a group of other comfort women, under the guidance and protection of the Task Force of Filipino Comfort Women and Asian Women Human Rights Council, sued the Japanese government for their crimes and were offered a small settlement from the Asian Women's Fund in 1995.[90] Many comfort women refused the Japanese government's minimal attempts at paying for their veterans' crimes. To this day, the Japanese government's blatant refusal to fully acknowledge their soldiers' past sexual crimes continues to be a topic of international debate for those concerned with human rights and war reparations.[91]

Maria Rosa Henson's roles as a female guerrilla, comfort woman, mother, daughter, and women's activist showcase the multitude of responsibilities that women, or "casualties of war," shouldered. Henson's narrative as a rape victim, turned survivor, turned activist, challenges the historical interpretation that women in war are powerless bodies. The women of this chapter, especially Henson and Culala, share and carry a gender-related cloud of shame. Culala is portrayed as a villainess, her accomplishments and role in the Huk resistance min-

---

90. Yuki Tanaka "Introduction," *Comfort Woman: A Filipina's Story of Prostitution and Slavery Under the Japanese Military,* New York: Rowman & Littlefield, 2017, p. xx, xxiii.
91. Atwood, ibid., p. 108.

imized to a supporting role, with the myth surrounding her execution serving as a warning to *pinays* who supposedly submit to their vanity. Henson's experiences as a comfort woman are associated with the stigma of losing one's feminine purity, and thus represent three of the casualties of female victimhood in war; social, psychological, and physical contamination. Both women and their experiences in traditional Filipino settings represent outliers during and after the war. Culala challenged the male hierarchy of leadership in the resistance, whereas Henson challenged intersecting gender and cultural stigmas associated with the purity of women's bodies. Both aggressively crossed boundaries limited to their sex and reconstructed notions of women's participation in war, thus making women visible actors rather than tallied casualties of war.

Protecting and safeguarding women's bodies was both a form of self-defense and patriotism. For *pinay guerrilleras*, the patriotism that fueled their dedication to the underground Huk resistance was inherently tied to the protection and safety of their womanhood. As patriotic liberators, Filipinas gained control over their bodies. Only when Filipinas possessed the means to defend themselves and oversee the conversations pertaining to their bodies, like Maria demonstrated, were Filipina soldiers of World War II considered controversial, unconventional, and simultaneously silenced, as evidenced by the blemished legacy of Culala's contribution to the Huk and the refusal of the Japanese government to publicly acknowledge the existence of comfort women.

Chapter 2. The Hearts of the Huk

Photographed above is a bronze statue dedicated to the Filipina comfort women. The statue was initially erected in 2017 and placed on Roxas Boulevard overlooking Manila Bay. However, soon after, the statue was taken down later in the spring of 2018 under President Duterte's orders as he did not want to "offend" Japanese relations.[92]

Pinays who served in the war were aware of the potential consequences and backlash they would receive stepping into the battlefield and wartime politics. The *guerrilleras* who wished to participate in the liberation of their country navigated their roles with more precaution, taking great care in balancing Filipino gender norms and expectations about Filipina femininity as they negotiated their guerrilla roles with their male peers. And it was

---

92. Gaea Katreena Cabico, "Gabriela Solons seek probe into removal of comfort woman statue," *PhilStar News*, last modified May 10th, 2018, last accessed December 28th, 2018, https://www.philstar.com/headlines/2018/05/10/1813942/gabriela-solons-seek-probe-removal-comfort-woman-statue.

these *pinays* who adhered to gendered cultural standards of beauty, femininity, and maternalism that became the preferred and more glamorous mainstays of what little history survived about Filipina war heroes.

Chapter 3

The Glamorous *Guerrilleras:* Amazons of the Pacific Theater

A training photograph of a Filipina Women's Auxiliary Corps in Manila. The first official Women's Auxiliary Service (WAS) was founded by Josefa Capistrano in Mindanao. The women pictured here were one of the first groups of Filipinas to train and serve as combat guerrillas, November 8th, 1942.[93]

---

93. Doc Snafu, "(USAFFE) (Far East) Guerrilla Movement, Philippines, 1942-1945," *EUCMH Exposition Blog*, last modified July 17th, 2015, last accessed August 15th, 2018, https://www.eucmh.com/2015/07/17/usaffe-far-east-guerrilla-movement-philippines-1942-1945/.

The uniqueness of the Filipina World War II experience is revealed by the bold and untold accounts of female-led insurgencies during the Japanese Occupation. Surviving oral accounts and rarely published histories of Filipina guerrilla soldiers describe them as knowledgeable in combat and strategy—equal to their male peers. Filipina guerrillas organized and commanded insurgent units over expansive terrain. They also conducted much of the spy and infiltration work needed to provide stable communication and supply networks for the Philippine Underground Resistance and the remnants of MacArthur's American Allied intelligence throughout the Philippine archipelago. Filipinas served as couriers for guerrillas, donated weapons and supplies, secretly housed and nursed Filipino and American POWs, and took up arms themselves. Filipinas of the resistance fought the Japanese on various fronts as *guerrilleras*, just as bravely as men did. Without their contributions, the liberation movement could quite possibly have failed.

Despite their valiance, the actions of women of color in the Pacific Theater are not as well-recorded as their male counterparts, frequently being subsumed by male-centric narratives of heroism, escape, and intrigue. Women who bravely fought within male-dominated insurgencies and the arena of war politics faced unique challenges and difficulties made more pressing by their gender, including the threats of capture, rape, torture, enemy fire, and death. Additionally, women experienced constant verbal consternation from their male peers born from gender-based anxieties.

Chapter 3. The Glamorous Guerrilleras: Amazons of the Pacific Theater

Claire Fuentes Phillips was an American whose first marriage was to a Filipino sailor. After their daughter was born, Phillips and her husband divorced and she found a job as part of an entertainment business in the Philippines. When the war broke out, Phillips decided to open a nightclub where she could use her singing and dancing skills to tease out military information from Japanese officers as they drank and enjoyed the nightly entertainment. As a guerrilla spy, she fed information to the local resistance and smuggled supplies to the POWS at the Santo Tomas Internment Camp with the money she raised from her nightclub. Phillips operated the nightclub in Manila and called it the Tsubaki Club. In her memoir, Phillips describes how her team of guerrilla spies, made up of Filipina/x hostesses, dancers (a Filipina transwoman by the name of Walterina Markova), and bar girls (by the names of Fely Corcuera, Flora, and Fahny), and waiters (one of whom Phillips only names as David) were able to tease out the most crucial information about the IJA's and Japanese Navy's locations, movements, and where and when they received their supplies. She was eventually captured by the Japanese and jailed at Fort Santiago. She survived the war and the month-long abuse from her interrogators. In the article above published in *The Philippines Mail*, Claire went on to receive the Asiatic-Pacific-Campaign Ribbon Award from General MacArthur for her contribution as a *guerrillera*, circa May 1945.[94]

Mrs. Fuentes Arrives From The Philippines

PORTLAND, OREGON — Mrs Claire Fuentes, wife of Mr. Manuel Fuentes, Assistant Superintendent of the Army Transport Service at Fort Mason, was the recipient of the Asiatic-Pacific Campaign Ribbon awarded by General MacArthur to civilians in the Philippines who by their courage

MRS. CLAIRE FUENTES

and intrepidity in helping the internees during the Japanese oppression in the Islands, facilitated the liberation of the Philippines. Mrs. Fuentes was jailed in Fort Santiago and tried by Japanese court martial, sentenced to prison and given by the Japanese Military all the maltreatment imaginable because of her connection with the underground resistance and because she helped the American internees in Santo Tomas. She arrived in this country early in May with her infant daughter Daine, and is at present vacationing with her parents in Portland, to join her husband later in San Francisco, California.

---

94. Staff writer, "Mrs. Fuentes Arrives from the Philippines," *The Philippines Mail*, May 1945, microfilm, John Steinbeck Public Library, Salinas, California.

As American studies scholar Denise Cruz describes in her book *Transpacific Femininities: The Making of the Modern Filipina*, wartime Filipinas who worked tirelessly in the ranks of the resistance movement, although deemed patriotic, were both underrepresented among their male peers and often designated to roles that matched familial conventions seen in traditional Filipino patriarchal households: as mothers, sisters, or caregivers. If Filipinas wished to liberate their country from Japanese occupation, they also had to risk the social criticisms of their male peers, who held steadfast to the *machismo* values exercised at nearly every rank and file of the underground resistance. Filipina guerrillas who took on leadership positions during the war, therefore, had to demonstrate and perform the preferred characteristics of the ideal Filipina to participate in the war and be deemed a Philippine patriot by their peers.

Many of the accounts of Filipina guerrillas that do survive—and are most celebrated—often emphasize the women who both represented ideal Filipina beauty standards of the period and took on the preferred characteristics of the attentive nurse, adoring mother, and lover. Although performing such an assemblage of roles is a daunting and incredible feat during wartime, it is also true that such roles upheld certain patriarchal values. However, there is a part of this story that is less well-known. Indeed, many of these "ideal" Filipina *guerrilleras* also contributed to the resistance in ways that challenged rather than appeased the patriarchy.

Chapter 3. The Glamorous Guerrilleras: Amazons of the Pacific Theater

The most revered of these *guerrilleras* were the military heroines, or "Filipina Amazons," who took it upon themselves to reform traditional standards of Philippine beauty, familial structure, and social patriarchy, whilst also conducting soldierly subterfuge and formulating battle strategies. These Filipina Amazons are often the most celebrated Filipinas in narratives written about the Philippines' fight against Japanese occupation, in part because they represent a perfect blend of wartime romanticism and culturally dominant notions of Filipino conventions of female beauty and grace. In their own ways, these glamorous guerrillas reshaped the notions of intra-ethnic gender relations and demonstrated outright women's capacities and major potential as community influencers and military leaders.

Colonel Yay Panlilio

> *"I wrote into my column advice for the women: 'Let your children look back and remember how their mothers faced the war'."*[95]
> —Colonel Yay Panlilio

As a trained journalist concerned with Filipino national politics and women's rights, Yay Panlilio's contributions to the early strands and waves of resistance drew heavily from her own grassroots ideologies. With a background

---

95. Yay Panlilio, *The Crucible: An Autobiography by Colonel Yay, Filipina American Guerrilla,* New Brunswick: Rutgers University Press, 1950.

A photograph of Panlilio at the Marking Guerrilla headquarters at the close of the war, circa 1945.[96]

in muckraking journalism, and as a politically savvy radio host turned *guerrillera*, Panlilio added layers of glamour, sensationalism, and long overdue sentiments of Filipino nationalist language to promote the goals of the guerrilla resistance. Her autobiography, *The Cruci-*

---

96. 17.21 Women, "Yay Panlilio," *Deskgram*, last modified July 2018, last accessed December 23rd, 2018, https://deskgram.net/explore/tags/yay-panlilio.

ble: An Autobiography by Colonel Yay, Filipina American Guerrilla, relays her daring military exploits during the war in a manner akin to an action-packed film. In combination with her *mestiza* looks and tumultuous love affair with the leader of the Marking Guerrillas, her autobiography paints a romanticized telling of the guerrilla movement that caters to the overemphasis, as scholar Denise Cruz argues, of the generalized roles and experiences of women during wartime.[97]

Yay Panlilio is one of the most celebrated female leaders of the resistance. Her personal autobiography remains the key written resource in terms of depicting the rare experiences of Filipina insurgents who held high military ranks. Panlilio, a biracial Filipino American *mestiza*, was revered by both the Filipino and American soldiers she oversaw. Her motherly treatment and command of her troops, her beauty as a fair-skinned, racially mixed *mestiza,* combined with her American and Filipino upbringing and her straddling of two cultural fronts in the Pacific Theater, made her the "ideal Filipina woman" of war. However, Panlilio's autobiography does not highlight her own achievements as a commander of male troops, or her other contributions to the war effort as an outspoken journalist, *guerrillera* spy, and Filipino patriot. Instead, her account of the war puts the efforts of men, like her love interest Colonel Marcos V. Agustin, front and center. Nonetheless, she often describes herself, perhaps without being

---

97. Denise Cruz, *Transpacific Femininities: The Making of the Modern Filipina,* Duke University Press, 2012, p. 175.

conscious of her tendencies to kowtow to Agustin's violent and ego-centric whims, as a leader of the Marking Guerrillas.

Her words and submissive intonations, found throughout her narrative of the war, may have, as Denise Cruz argues, been the only way to attract audiences to listen to her story, by painting herself as a damsel running into the trenches of war, finding love, and in the end, running off victorious and married to the man she supported on the front lines.[98] Whatever Panlilio's intentions were in relegating herself to the traditional and overly romanticized role as lover and dutiful wife, her autobiography remains a valuable account of *pinay* history. Her written account is a primary source that highlights her role as a colonel and encounters with other Filipina guerrillas, showcasing the existence of military-engaged women and leaders while further demonstrating, in the manner in which she chose her words, the various gendered barriers strong women faced head-on in male-centric war-torn terrains.

> "Filipinos will die for love. Americans will die for principle. I am half-and-half. I die the same way."[99]
>
> —Yay Panlilio

---

98. Ibid., pp. 167-178.
99. Denise Cruz, ed., Yay Panlilio, *The Crucible: An Autobiography by Colonel Yay, Filipina American Guerrilla,* Rutgers University Press, 2009, p. 63.

Yay Panlilio was born and raised in Denver, Colorado, in 1913. She was a *mestiza*, a woman of mixed race; her father was Irish-American, and her mother was Filipina. Panlilio, proud of her mixed heritage, described herself as a woman who encapsulated both cultures. Yay would eventually leave the United States as a teenager and embarked on pursuing a career as a serious radio news correspondent and journalist in the Philippines.[100]

Panlilio worked in Manila as a reporter for the *Philippines Herald* before the war. Later, when the threat of invasion was imminent, she became sworn in as a U.S. Intelligence agent. When the war broke out in 1941, she requested to leave Manila and head with the army to Bataan. Her letters of request were denied and she was told to "stick around" in order to continue reporting any Japanese movement in occupied Manila.[101] After consistent refusals from U.S. Intelligence chief officers like Captain Ralph Keeler, Panlilio decided she would practice her own style of resistance and declared herself a guerrilla.

Panlilio's initial guerrilla tactics involved her use of familiar news media positions to facilitate propaganda against the Japanese. She used her radio broadcasts via KZRH Manila Radio to send coded messages hinting at information about nearby Japanese activity to the newly forming resistance movement.[102] Her messages were so cryptic that even General MacArthur was known to

---

100. Panlilio, *The Crucible*, p. ix.
101. Denise Cruz, ed., Yay Panlilio, ibid., p. 7, 8.
102. Ibid., p. 12.

become frustratingly concerned with Panlilio's loyalties, not knowing what to make of Panlilio's radio efforts, especially as the Japanese directly monitored her every move and broadcast.[103]

While working with KZRH, the Japanese secured intel regarding the person who managed the radio broadcasting. One of her acquaintances at the station became a recruit for the Japanese Military Intelligence, a man by the name of Taki. Over time Panlilio gave him false information about the whereabouts of American and Filipino rebels and guerrilla sympathizers, hoping she could bide enough time to put the Imperial Japanese Army off the scent of the Allies and guerrilla resistance in the Philippines. Playing a double agent was risky, but *pinay* guerrillas like Panlilio were willing to sacrifice life and limb to bring about the liberation of the Philippines, knowing very well that torture, rape, and the murder of innocent relatives were the possible consequences of their actions.

Panlilio was for some time able to avoid detection, but eventually, Japanese suspicions led to attempts at arresting her. Panlilio, having no time to lose, left Manila while in disguise with the help of sympathetic locals and other resistance contacts. They provided Panlilio with freshly laundered women's clothing, makeup, and different male guides to disguise herself with in order to survive from one checkpoint to the next.[104] Yay escaped to the mountains and would hide in the hut of a farmer by the name of Igi, but soon after she became afflicted with malaria.

---

103. Cruz, *Transpacific Femininities*, pp. 169-179.
104. Panlilio, *The Crucible*, pp. 12-15.

Nevertheless, fate would ensure that Panlilio would soon be called into service once more. While Panlilio was recovering from malaria, guerrillas under Colonel Agustin stumbled upon her location whilst searching for a secure place to hide. Inside Igi's hut, they found the journalist-turned-guerrilla-resistance-fighter-in-the-making resting inside. Despite her illness, Panlilio was ready and willing to contribute something to the resistance.

Fearing that a Japanese patrol would find them, Panlilio urged the men to hide in the surrounding area and recuperate in order to avoid capture. These men were Marking's Guerillas, a unit of resistance fighters led by Marcos V. Agustin.[105] From that point forward, Yay became an essential asset and a member of Marcos'—also known as Marking's—guerrilla resistance.[106]

For two years she would live in the jungle and fight alongside the guerrillas. She survived a bout of malaria, among other jungle-related ailments, and countless injuries from Japanese attacks. Unfortunately, Yay would fall into an abusive and demanding relationship with Colonel Marking while going through the emotional pains of being separated from her three children from a previous marriage, while they were kept hostage by the Japanese.[107] All of these experiences were compounded by the gendered guerrilla hierarchies she as a woman faced within the secluded and male-dominated total war environment.

---

105. Ibid., p. 15.
106. Ibid., p. 21.
107. Ibid., p. 10.

The official flag of the Marking Guerrillas as depicted by surviving veterans and their families' accounts.[108]

Yay dealt with the sharp and stubborn tongues of male guerrillas who despised the idea of taking orders from a woman. One guerrilla by the name of Ming Javellana lobbed an underhanded comment at Yay after she gave orders for sleeping arrangements, complaining that "We fight. We don't eat. We don't sleep... And now we take orders from a woman."[109] Yay understood the gen-

---

108. Marking's Guerrillas were established in the Sierra Madre Mountains under Colonel Hugh Straughn, a Spanish American War veteran. Eventually, Marking's Guerrillas became an independent organization when Straughn was captured and killed in August of 1943. Marking's Guerrillas were seen as ruthless by both the Japanese soldiers as well as those who opposed their rank and were known to engage in open conflict with the Hunters ROTC Guerrillas. Watawat. net, "The Wha-Chi and Other Guerrilla Groups and Units," *Watawat: Flags and Symbols of the Pearl of the Orient Seas*, last modified 2017, last accessed December 17th, 2018, http://www.watawat.net/the-wha-chi--and-other-guerrilla-groups-and-units.html.
109. Panlilio, *The Crucible*, p. 15, 19.

Chapter 3. The Glamorous Guerrilleras: Amazons of the Pacific Theater

dered biases men had of women, especially in wartime, believing they were a detriment to the resistance, possibly even as detrimental as a double agent. Marking's men, Yay described, "hid their disgust behind blank faces: They could see dainty horns coming out from my temples, a forked tail curl about one ankle."[110] Being able to hold one's chin high while under Japanese fire and taking bitter sexist insults from one's own "comrades" on a regular basis made the life of a *guerrillera* a personal and gendered war zone; a war zone where women's social marginalization became magnified, multiplied, and compounded with the daily terror of total war.

The desperate mental state, as well as the harrowing physical toll experienced by constantly malnourished guerrilla fighters, who had to be ready at any moment for orders to raid a Japanese camp, or to pick up and evade a surprise Japanese attack, are viscerally described by Panlilio's journalistic flair and knack for writing in her memoir. Panlilio describes being in such close proximity to the Japanese army that she always had to be in the mindset to be prepared to shoot herself in order to avoid capture and interrogation because she feared she would divulge too much critical information under torture.[111] At one point, while escaping enemy fire, Panlilio describes how she and the remnants of a group of Marking's Guerillas' only chance of survival meant climbing down a cliff face, without any of the necessary equipment to do so safely. After this attack, Panlilio and her men survived starva-

---

110. Ibid., pp. 18-20.
111. Ibid., p. 200.

tion and being rooted out by the Japanese thanks to the kindness and support of the local villagers they encountered.[112]

Panlilio's detailed autobiography provides an excellent depiction of life as a guerrilla during the Japanese occupation, and in addition shows how involved women were in the resistance movement, even outside of the Hukbalahap party. Panlilio's mentions of several 'girl fighters' that she came across provide first account evidence of the Filipina *guerrilleras* who fought alongside their male peers. In particular, Panlilio praised the *guerrillera*, Captain Trinidad Diaz. Panlilio described Diaz's contribution to the underground resistance as essential to the momentum of the movement because similar to Celia Mariano Pomeroy and Commander Simeona Punsalan, she took on the task of recruiting informants while creating her own militant intelligence network that thwarted the local Japanese in her area of Binangonan.

Yay's brief account of Diaz praises not only her bravery but her cleverness in using her connections as a courier and cashier at her community's local cement factory to effectively conduct her undercover missions.[113] Panlilio noted that Diaz's Home Guard unit patrolled her community's region and attacked Japanese soldiers. Diaz and her men hid the bodies of the soldiers in cement mixers to conceal any tracks leading to the efforts of her guerrilla branch. Diaz and her home guard of guerrillas also provided supplies such as food and ammunition

---

112. Ibid., pp. 74-78.
113. Ibid., p. 31.

Chapter 3. The Glamorous Guerrilleras: Amazons of the Pacific Theater

to Marking's guerrillas through the network of contacts Diaz established.

Eventually, the Japanese caught Diaz, tied her up, tortured her relentlessly (hanging her upside down, lashing her, and burning her), and executed her, but not before Diaz's *guerrillera* strategizing and networking galvanized further morale for the resistance.[114] Without Yay's humble mention of fellow *guerrilleras* like Captain Diaz, her sacrifices, like those of many other *pinays* who joined the resistance, might have been lost.

An original copy of a later edition of Panlilio's wartime memoir, *The Crucible*, with photographs of both her and her ex-husband Colonel Marking. The cover centers attention on Marking despite the wartime memoir being firmly based on Panlilio's experiences.[115]

---

114. Ibid., p. 30.
115. PinoyKollector, "Marking," eBay Books, last accessed December 25th, 2018, http://www.pinoycollector.com/ebay/books/March2008/.

WOMAN GUERRILLA CHIEF LAUDS ANGELENO OFFICER

It was a heroic crowd that sprang from vivid memories in the quiet hotel room.

There was the taciturn, brooding schoolmaster, who taught the Moros in peace and led and inspired them in war; there was the gallant American officer, who shared the privations and small fare of the guerrillas, and there were the guerrillas themselves, 200,000 of them, who came out of the barrios to unite their strength against the Japanese.

Had Price on Her Head

All of them were, and those still alive are, the friends of Mrs. Yay Panlilio, Filipina guerrilla leader, chief of staff of Marking's Fil-Americans, an army of almost a quarter of a million, who harried the Japs from the hills of the Philippines, pledged, the visitor said, to resist the enemy to the end.

Although she had a price on her head and was long separated from her three children, Edward, 9; Curtis, 3, and Rae, 12; although she suffered hardships and was frequently in serious danger, she preferred to talk about others rather than herself in her room in the Baltimore, particularly about a Los Angeles Army officer, whose name cannot be disclosed because of censorship regulations, and Edward M. Kudner, the island schoolteacher.

The Los Angeles officer was stated by the visitor to have executed so splendidly his work as liaison officer with the guerrillas that he had been praised by four generals, headed by Gen. MacArthur, and by Gen. Carlos P. Romulo, Philippine Resident Commissioner.

He Kept the Faith

"Not every captain gets praised by four generals in a row," exclaimed Mrs. Panlilio.

"Some of his assignments were almost impossible to fulfill," she said, "yet, he managed, working 18 to 20 hours a day for a week at a stretch, month after month,

holding the guerrillas steady and waiting for orders, answering headquarters' questions with accurately compiled data in less time than was demanded—never complaining, never loafing, never doubting that the people back home in America were with him and all those like him when the rain poured cold and heavy, when he almost starved, but didn't quit."

Kudner, the visitor stated, in nearly 20 years of teaching won the love and confidence of the Moros, and, despite the unpredictable nature of the Moros, he was always safe among them.

She Was Born in Denver

Of herself, Mrs. Panlilio said that she was born in Denver and that she is half Filipina and half Irish. She went to the Islands when she was 18 and had been there 14 years when she was liberated, working during the years before the war on a newspaper in Manila.

Her three children, she said, had all seen Japanese cruelty.

Mrs. Panlilio plans to visit her mother in Auburn, Cal., before resuming her activities in behalf of Filipinos.

SAFE FROM JAPS—Mrs. Yay Panlilio, Filipino guerrilla leader, relaxes in Los Angeles with her children after fighting Japanese. From left to right, Edward, 9; Mrs. Panlilio; Curtis, 3, and Rae, 12. All escaped harm.

L.A. Times — August 1945

Article and L.A. Times clipping discussing Panlilio's war efforts, her *mestiza* background, and her motherly devotion to her family life.[116]

---

116. This article is about Mrs. Yay Panlilio, who was a Filipino guerrilla leader, who helped the U.S. in their fight against Japan. The emphasis of depicting Yay as a mother and supportive guerrilla soldier rather than as her role as a colonel are the central themes of the short *L.A. Times* piece by the American author George Miller. *L.A. Times* August 1945. *L.A. Times* August 1945, "Mrs. Yay Panlilio," *Nehalem Valley Historical Society Online Archive*, accessed December 18th, 2018, http://nehalemvalleyhistory.org/omeka/items/show/495.

Chapter 3. The Glamorous Guerrilleras: Amazons of the Pacific Theater

Panlilio's experiences as a *guerrillera* serve as an example of the extent to which women were at the mercy of men's physical and verbal treatment, even among the slightly more egalitarian guerrilla units. Her relationship with the guerrilla commander, Marking, was both abusive and manipulative, yet, nevertheless, she remained loyal to him and supported him emotionally and militarily, eventually marrying him (they would later divorce). While many of the guerrillas under her command treated her with respect, some referring to her as 'mammy,' other officers became deeply resentful of her leadership position. Rather than acknowledging her skill sets as a multilingual and devoted journalist, intelligence officer, and soldier, some men in Marking's guerrillas, particularly out of contempt of being led by a female officer, accused her of securing her position as colonel as a result of her sexual relations with Colonel Marcos Agustin.

In popular Philippine narratives and film productions after the war, like *Cry Freedom* (1959), Yay is still remembered for her dramatized wartime romance with Agustin, labeled as a "girl guerrilla," and described as a secondary, supportive, figure overshadowed by Agustin's personality as a war hero. She would return to the United States alone to raise her three children and publish her wartime memoir in 1950. In 1951, Colonel Yay was awarded the U.S. Medal of Freedom with a silver palm. And although her life and achievements are often constrained to the narrative that she was a doting mother, romanticized "girl guerrilla" persona, and an aide to the egocentric Colonel Marcos Agustin, Panlilio was, in actuality, a female literary and militant powerhouse in her own right.

Kumander Liwayway, a.k.a. Remedios Gomez

Another woman who embodied the ultra-feminine Filipina archetype while also exhibiting aggressive military prowess was Remedios Gomez. Known to wear lipstick and pristine get-ups while brandishing her weapons with polished nails and fashionable hair updos, Gomez was the epitome of Filipina beauty: a renowned beauty pageant barrio queen with brains and confidence to boot. She and her family became guerrillas after her father was tortured and executed by the Japanese in 1942.[117] She was given the code name Liwayway, and, like other guerrilla women before her, was assigned to work as a medic. She would soon rise through the ranks, driven by her desire to exact revenge against the Japanese for her father's death, and was assigned the posts of commander over Squadron 3-V and chief of the Military Provision Division of Central Luzon.[118]

In the Battle of Kamansi, she and her squad faced a larger Japanese force and succeeded in driving them back long after the other guerrilla squadrons had fled. As an officer, she also faced the endless task of providing for her men, which consisted of frequent travel to and from villages trying to rally sympathy and support for the resis-

---

117. Lanzona, *Amazons of the Huk Rebellion*, p. 152.
118. Ibid., p. 153, 154.

tance. Her men saw her as "a fearless and courageous leader unafraid to die."[119] Although Huk communist ideology defined passion, honor, dignity, and vengeance as strictly masculine emotions, Liwayway was seen by her male Huk comrades as capable of embodying both traditionally effeminate and traditionally masculine characteristics.[120] Indeed, her male comrades would often confront her and question her habits of putting lipstick on and wearing getups associated with social functions rather than battle. When one of her male peers, a man by the name of Katapatan, jested and insulted her with sexual innuendos, Liwayway challenged him to a duel, the result of which solidified her position as a Huk woman leader.[121]

Her Huk *guerrillera* comrades, like Commander Simeona Punsalan-Tapang (aka Kumander Guerrero), later on in life fondly remembered Liwayway's "feminine virtues":

> "Kumander Liwayway was truly beautiful and made us all wait while she put on make-up and polished her nails."[122]
>
> —Commander Simeona Punsalan

---

119. Tonette Orejas, "Liwayway: Warrior Who Wore Lipstick in Gun Battles," *Inquirer.Net*, last modified May 17th, 2014, last accessed December 19th, 2018, https://newsinfo.inquirer.net/602758/liwayway-warrior-who-wore-lipstick-in-gun-battles.
120. Lanzona, *Amazons of the Huk Rebellion*, p. 174.
121. The specific details of the duel remain unknown. See Andrew G. Gomez, *Kumander Liwayway: Joan of Ark of the Philippines, Based on the True Story of Remedios Gomez-Paraiso,* Central Book Supply, 2009.
122. Tonette Orejas, "Last Living Woman Huk Leader Gets Pension Back," ibid. Interview with Commander Simeona Punsalan, "Kumander

Liwayway's embodiment of the Philippine feminine archetype served as her way of displaying her pride as a Filipino woman who took charge of traditional gender tropes and transformed them into emblems of female leadership. She would continue to fight for the safety and inclusion of the Philippine peasants and farmers in the newly established Philippine Republic as a Huk underground resistance leader. She was caught twice by the Philippine Constabulary, and her husband and brother were killed by the new government. She was eventually released and cleared of her charges but was always kept under close surveillance throughout the Cold War for her associations with the Communist Party. She died at the age of 95 in 2014, but her legacy as a Huk *guerrillera* who fought for her people's liberation on two fronts (World War II and post-war Philippine state formation) would be memorialized in her biography, written by her younger brother in 2009, and again in historian Vina Lanzona's book, *Amazons of the Huk Rebellion: Gender, Sex, and Revolution in the Philippines*.

Josefa Borromeo Capistrano

Another Filipina trailblazer and powerhouse was Josefa Capistrano. Capistrano founded the Philippines' first Women's Auxiliary Service (WAS) in Mindanao. A Fil-

---

Guerrero of San Simon," last modified June 20th, 2014, last accessed December 19th, 2018, https://plus.google.com/+JenniferBichara/posts/MbCuptx3dK1.

Chapter 3. The Glamorous Guerrilleras: Amazons of the Pacific Theater

One of the surviving photographs of *guerrillera* Josefa Capistrano, founder of the Philippine Women's Auxiliary Corps.[123]

ipina-Chinese *mestiza* who was born to a family with prestigious political ties, Capistrano, like Yay, was a free-thinking Filipina ahead of her time. She strove to train and establish a purely female unit that would be recognized as an official unit of the Philippines Military.[124] The performance and skill of the WAS served as just one of the many landmark advances in women's rights and social presence in modern Philippines' history. Capistrano's WAS numbered three thousand militarily trained women skilled in combat, small industries (making bullets, textiles, bandages), nursing, and handling covert

---
123. "The 10 Most Incredible Filipina Warriors of World War II," ibid.
124. John Keats, *They Fought Alone: A True Story of an American Hero*, Echo Point Books and Media, 2015, p. 221, 245.

operations—particularly as spies—for both the American Allies and Filipino guerrilla networks.[125]

For Capistrano, all countrymen and women, from any class or background, were valuable assets to the resistance and the new Philippine Republic that Capistrano believed would come as a result of the liberation efforts of the guerrillas. On Mindanao, Capistrano exercised this belief, being assigned to lead and organize the "lay people," including women.[126] Capistrano's belief in women's capabilities set her apart from those Filipinos who thought that women should be relegated to more traditional labor roles. Her beliefs when put into practice also aided the resistance's efforts against the Japanese, who had a gendered and limited perception of women's potential as subversives. Capistrano's belief in women's subversive capacity gave the resistance an advantage in the war, so long as they were given the opportunity—as Capistrano believed they should be—to contribute in ways that went beyond being a sideline "supporter."

> "Without the help of the people of the country, a guerrilla organization is doomed to fail."[127]
> —Josefa Capistrano

---

125. Evelyn Mallillin Jamboy, *The Resistance Movement in Lanao, 1942-1945*, Coordination Center of Research and Development MSU-Iligan Institute of Technology, 2006, p. 74.
126. Miguel Anselmo Bernad, *History Against the Landscape: Personal and Historical Essays About the Philippines*, Solidaridad Publishing House, 1968, p. 41.
127. The Philippine Natural Historical Society, *The Journal of History: Volume 57*, Philippine Natural Historical Society, 2011, p. 253.

Chapter 3. The Glamorous Guerrilleras: Amazons of the Pacific Theater

Capistrano was aware of the limited roles and opportunities Filipina women had in their households and communities, but, unlike her commanders and fellow male guerrillas, she foresaw the potential of women's inclusion in the liberation front, and more broadly in the Philippine Republic. Her female guerrillas successfully worked alongside Commander Wendell Fertig's guerrilla units in Mindanao throughout the war, proving to both American and Philippine military commands that women could match men in battle and patriotic fervor.

Despite the success and inclusion of Capistrano's female-led war industries and military units, the depiction of Capistrano's physical *mestiza* beauty received more notoriety than her capacity as a guerrilla leader. Wendell Fertig, the famous American military engineer and commander of Filipino and American guerrillas in Mindanao, made sure to downplay Capistrano's military leadership in his autobiographical account made during the war, always referring to her as Nick Capistrano's "lovely wife."[128] At other points, she was described as "a *mestiza* of lustrous beauty whose skin had that creamy tone that only the slims of highborn Chinese have. Josefa always looked clean and delicate as a flower at dawn."[129] Like other depictions of *pinay guerrilleras*, Fertig highlighted Capistrano's beauty as a *mestiza*, her family's affluence, and her ties to her esteemed husband rather than designating her vital role as a spearheading

---

128. Nick Capistrano was a wealthy lumber owner. See Keats, *They Fought Alone* p. 388.
129. Keats, *They Fought Alone*, p. 130.

organizer and leader in her own right among the Mindanao guerrillas.[130]

Long after the war passed, Capistrano continued to argue for her female unit's recognition as an official branch of the Philippine Army. Thanks to Capistrano's headstrong perseverance in proving women's capabilities, particularly in instances of total war, Filipinas were allowed a foot in the door of post-war Philippines and were allowed to expand both their career choices and their responsibilities as Philippine citizens. On a par with men, Filipinas were seen as just as able in protecting their country and bear the official badge of a warrior and patriotic soldier. Capistrano's legacy included her contribution to the war as a *guerrillera* and organizer of her female guerrilla units, culminating in the formation of the WAS as an official branch of the Philippine Military Armed Forces. It would be renamed the Women's Auxiliary Corps in 1963.[131]

Nieves Fernandez

While Capistrano and Panlilio were praised and remembered for traditional notions of Filipina mestiza beauty, other popular *guerrillera* narratives preserved were those

---

130. Ibid., p. 210, 420.
131. William B. Depasupil, "Women's Auxiliary Corps Unmanned After 50 Years," *The Manila Times*, last modified July 5th, 2013, last accessed August 2nd, 2017, http://www.manilatimes.net/womens-auxiliary-corps-unmanned-after-50-years/16088/.

Chapter 3. The Glamorous Guerrilleras: Amazons of the Pacific Theater

Fernandez is photographed here demonstrating to an American soldier how to effectively disable a Japanese soldier with the Philippine long knife, the bolo. Circa November 7th, 1944.[132]

of women who held other attributes associated with the ideal Filipina matriarch. The other aspect of Filipina womanhood valued by traditional gender norms included the role of the motherly teacher. Nieves Fernandez was one such female guerrilla that embodied the strong Filipina patriot and military leader while choosing the lifeway of a maternal preceptor. As one of the

---

132. Rare Historical Photos, "Captain Nieves Fernandez shows to an American soldier how she used her long knife to silently kill Japanese soldiers during occupation, 1944," *Rare Historical Photos: Southeast Asia*, last modified June 21st, 2014, last accessed December 27th, 2018, https://rarehistoricalphotos.com/captain-nieves-fernandez-1944/.

lesser-known Filipina guerrilla leaders of the Pacific War, her story, like Kumander Liwayway's, has either been retold with romanticized wartime embellishments or been nearly glossed over into complete obscurity.

Few resources document Fernandez's guerrilla activity. Those that survive include sparse recollections of the soldiers who fought alongside her and the local communities of Tacloban on the island of Leyte that she sought to protect. Before the outbreak of the war, Fernandez lived as a simple school teacher.[133] Her first physical altercation with the Japanese that pushed her to take a more aggressive stance to defend her homeland involved a scuffle where the lives of her students were threatened. Imperial Japanese soldiers had gone through Fernandez's town and came around to the small school where she taught, threatening to take away her students. In the heat of the scuffle, she retaliated by shooting at the Japanese soldiers with her homemade shotgun.[134] Described as a skilled marksman and bolo fighter, Fernandez gained the respect of native locals, led her own unit of men into battle, and was so successful in taking out Japanese patrols that the Japanese stationed in Tacloban placed a hefty 10,000-peso bounty on her.[135]

---

133. FMA Academy, "International Women's Day—Nieves Fernandez," *Filipino Martial Arts Academy: Certified and Comprehensive Instruction in the Filipino Martial Arts*, last modified March 8th, 2016, last accessed August 15th, 2018, http://fmaacademy.com/tag/captain-nieves/.
134. Marc V., "14 Amazing Filipina Heroines You Don't Know But Should," ibid.
135. FMA Academy, "International Women's Day—Nieves Fernandez."

Fernandez, like other guerrillas throughout the Philippines, relied on makeshift weapons such as the "paltik" (a homemade shotgun made of gas pipes), bolos (a large single-edged knife), homemade grenades (casings filled with old nails) and whatever items she and the one hundred and ten guerrillas under her could pilfer from the Japanese.[136] Fernandez lived until her nineties, living the last years of her life in Tacloban. The sole surviving pieces of evidence depicting her heroics are a photograph and a small 1944 American newspaper article depicting her guerrilla contributions prior to the arrival of General MacArthur on Leyte.[137]

Wartime always produces a desperate and immoral landscape. Women in the Philippines faced additional threats compared to their male peers, which stemmed specifically from the traditional assumptions regarding the weakness associated with women. Women and children, throughout many world histories of war and conquest, experienced violent acts of subjugation including rape, molestation, torture, physical and psychological abuse, and enslavement. Asian women throughout the Pacific Theater were forced, under terrifying circum-

---

136. Unknown author, "School Ma'am Led Guerrillas On Leyte," *Lewiston Daily Sun*, October 26th, 1944, last accessed August 15th, 2018, http://www.michaeldsellers.com/blog/2017/02/11/looking-for-info-on-captain-nieves-fernandez-wwii-guerrilla-leader-in-leyte-philippines/.
137. Michael Sellers, "Captain Nieves Fernandez—WWII Guerrilla Leader in Leyte, Philippines," last modified February 11th, 2017, last accessed August 15th, 2018, http://www.michaeldsellers.com/blog/2017/02/11/looking-for-info-on-captain-nieves-fernandez-wwii-guerrilla-leader-in-leyte-philippines/.

stances, to obey the Japanese invaders or suffer the consequences of war. Yet despite the atrocities committed against Filipinas by the Japanese Imperial Army, Filipinas like Nieves Fernandez still chose to fight bravely alongside their male counterparts. Their histories reveal that women were more than able, efficient, and self-driven leaders of the guerrilla resistance, regardless of the risks.

The "extraordinary" Filipina Amazons of war discussed in this chapter are those *pinays* who matched a specific and preferred archetype—that of the ideal Filipina war hero. The most celebrated women of the guerrilla resistance aligned with the desired physical beauty standards, maternalistic personalities, and traditional gender roles and conventions afforded to Filipino women at mid-century. *Pinays* who straddled these immense expectations in gender performance within patriarchal war zones, like *guerrillera* leaders Panlilio and Liwayway, survive in the historical memory of the war-torn Philippines as untouchable, ultra-feminine, modest, and pure; all the ideal standards expected of a humble acquiescent Filipina patriot.

However, at the same time, emphasizing such exceptional Filipina guerrilla heroines denies equal recognition to other *pinays* who were more "ordinary" in terms of their beauty, social class, and family lineage, and are not always depicted within the gendered backdrop of war as mothering supportive figures or caregiving sisters. Only recently have we recovered the accomplishments of the "ordinary" *pinay* guerrillas discussed in the

Chapter 3. The Glamorous Guerrilleras: Amazons of the Pacific Theater

following chapter. These were Filipina heroines whose narratives lack the glamour associated with romantic Filipino and American notions of the *mestiza* traditional beauty. The dichotomy of their humble "ordinariness" and extraordinary wartime experiences demonstrates the silent and less visible ways in which *pinays* obtained female empowerment. Taken together, the politically radical and vocal *guerrillera* Huks discussed earlier, the glamorous *pinay* Amazons highlighted in this chapter, and the everyday Filipinas detailed in the following chapter, represent a new standard—a new mold—for the model Filipina patriot.

Chapter 4

Filipina American Veterans: Recovering the Extraordinary Feats of the Ordinary Pinays

Focusing on the untouchable heroes who match all of the famous literature's great expectations and depictions of war, liberty, and adventure often narrows our vision and hinders our ability to see all those champions who opted for a more "ordinary" life. This includes the women who came from less prominent lineages, who did not don the ultra-feminine Filipina mystique, were non-*mestizas*, and who left behind their espionage missions to make a home and raise their families. These "ordinary" women, who could so easily be our neighbors, aunts, or grandmothers, are too often overlooked in our search for heroes.

The *pinay* guerrillas who survived the war and laid down their weapons found that they were forced to return to social conditions similar to what they had known before the war. Marriage, family, and possibly continuing one's education were the routes available to Filipinas still restricted to the patriarchal cultural norms that the Philippines at mid-century embraced. They immigrated,

An advertisement channeling the maternalistic grace and peaceful aura associated with Filipino women's traditional roles as gentle matriarchs who oversaw the Filipino recruited troops training in California. The ad was sponsored by the Filipino American fraternal organization, the Caballeros De Dimas-Alang, printed in a local Filipino American Newspaper in Los Angeles, circa 1940s. Filipino American Collections, Courtesy of the Cultural Center of Guadalupe.[138]

lived normal lives, married and had children, and did not discuss their efforts until decades later. Even then they still argued that their roles were small and that the men who commanded them or delegated and oversaw

---

138. Filipino American Collections, Courtesy of the Cultural Center of Guadalupe, California.

their actions were the real heroes, unable to see themselves in a similar light. In truth, these women were assigned to protect families, sent coded messages, and worked as undercover agents scoping Japanese military stations. They participated in the resistance despite the risk it posed to themselves in the form of rape and torture, and did all these tasks despite the extent to which their actions endangered their families and friends. Indeed, because these women had families, they often had much more at stake. If they were caught, they risked shaming their family name. And yet, despite these risks, these women still met the war head-on.

Josefina Veluya-Guerrero

The "ordinary" women who thrived within the resistance were often the antithesis of the classic Filipina Amazon. Unlike the Amazons, who were worshipped for their *mestiza* attributes, ordinary Filipina *guerrilleras* were often marginalized because others believed them to be substandard, either physically or otherwise. Ironically, such shallow assumptions and marginalization often made these women more effective operatives and spies. Indeed, those relegated to the bottom rung of the social caste system in traditional colonial Southeast Asian communities, such as the indigenous groups (for example the *Igorots, Aetas*), landless peasants, or even those afflicted with physical or medical handicaps, could more easily travel from one town to another province or barrio,

Photographed above is *guerrillera* Josefina Guerrero posing for her carnet (international customs/international documents) photo, she was also known as "The Leper Spy," circa 1970.[139]

often left untouched by both enemy surveillance and the locals' attention because they were not seen as potential threats. One such individual, Josefina Veluya-Guerrero, who suffered from leprosy, used social ostracization to her advantage. Her isolated status allowed her to operate under Japanese radar after they invaded and captured Manila in 1942.[140]

Throughout the Philippines in the nineteenth and early twentieth centuries, lepers were excluded from social and public spaces. Filipina/o lepers were forced to carry signs stating that they had the disease. Others

---

139. Photograph of Josefina Guerrero, from the Hoover Institution Archives, Stanford, California.
140. Ben Montgomery. *Leper Spy: The Story of an Unlikely Hero of World War II,* Chicago Review Press, 2016, p. 20.

were forced to carry a bell on their body and clothes so that people could hear them approaching, giving them the time to flee and avoid "catching" the illness themselves. For other unfortunate souls afflicted with the condition, they were placed in "leper colonies" away from the rest of society so as to isolate the disease.[141]

Fortunately, Josefina was able to avoid being sent to a leper colony, receiving private treatments that kept her illness secret from her community.[142] However, when the Japanese attacked Manila, she was unable to continue receiving treatment and her condition began to deteriorate. With both her country afflicted by Japan's occupation and her body in dire straits, Josefina believed that she did not have much time left to live. Her sense of desperation, combined with the isolation she felt as a leper, and the dwindling hopes she had for her country's liberation, influenced her decision to join the resistance. She decided to—instead of allowing her condition to define her remaining time left—use the stigma associated with her illness to her advantage to avoid Japanese suspicion and contact and support the resistance.

Josefina's primary role in the resistance was as a courier. She carried intel from Manila to guerrilla camps stationed in the forests and mountain provinces, often hiding the notes twisted and wrapped within her hair as she styled it into a chignon or hair bun.[143] Without proper treatment, Josefina's illness became more visible,

---

141. Ibid., Chapter: "Volunteer."
142. Ibid., p. 26.
143. Ibid., Chapter: "Spies."

which she continued to use to her advantage. Japanese guards refused to search her once they saw the "leper marks" on her arms and rushed her through checkpoints out of fear of contracting leprosy themselves. As more American soldiers began to make some headway in infiltrating Philippine shores, Josefina's courier operations extended beyond the guerrilla camps to working directly with USAFFE.

One of her more dangerous assignments included mapping enemy gun placements. Her maps allowed American bomber pilots to strategically coordinate aerial attacks, which significantly weakened Japanese cover and artillery stations. Josefina went to great lengths to obtain much-needed intel, so much so that she made a thirty-five-mile trek under heavy fire to give the Allies a map of the exact locations of Japanese mines and traps in the area.[144] Josefina's roles as courier and cartographer served as great assets to the liberation of the Philippines. Her sacrifices, bravery, and overall impact as a resistance intelligence officer challenged, if only temporarily, the social "taint" attached to leprosy.

After the war, the United States government awarded Guerrero with the Medal of Freedom with a silver palm and welcomed her to the United States with a visitor's permit to live in a leprosarium in Louisiana, where she received treatment for her condition and eventually was

---

144. Colette Bancroft, "Ben Montgomery's 'Leper Spy' An Extraordinary True Story of WWII," *Tampa Bay Times*, last accessed December 25th, 2018, https://www.tampabay.com/features/books/ben-montgomerys-leper-spy-an-extraordinary-true-story-of-wwii/2294553.

able to keep her disease dormant.[145] Although she faced multiple threats of deportation, Josefina was eventually given citizenship, and lived a simple life in San Francisco and then finally in Washington D.C., where she would settle permanently.

Joey, as she would be called by her American friends, would never speak about her espionage and heroic efforts as a *guerrillera*. To Joey's friends and neighbors in her later years, she was known only as a "humble and plain woman."[146] She lived the last leg of her elderly career as a well-to-do American citizen who worked for seventeen years as an usher for the Kennedy Center. She died in 1996 at the age of sixty-eight, leaving little to no remnants of her wartime memories as a "leper spy." It would take a trained and renowned journalist named Ben Montgomery to piece together her turbulent life in the Philippines and her quiet post-guerrilla career in the United States, revealing what we now know about this extraordinary "ordinary" woman.

Corporal Magdalena Leones

Magdalena Leones is another Filipina guerrilla who dared the trek across the Pacific after the war in search of a simple life and humbler career. Born in the mountain

---

145. Cristina DC Pastor, "How the WWII Hero Josefina Guerrero Struggled with Deportation," *The FilAm: A Magazine for Filipino Americans in New York*, last modified November 26th, 2016, last accessed December 20th, 2018, https://thefilam.net/archives/22758.
146. Montgomery. *Leper Spy*, Chapter: "Everything Is in Readiness."

Photographed above is Magdalena Leones, one of the highest honored Filipina American World War II veterans, circa 1940s.[147]

province of Kalinga of Northern Luzon, Magdalena grew up in a Protestant household that was soon turned upside down by the war. In 1942, when the Imperial Japanese Army invaded the Philippines, Magdalena was captured and jailed by the enemy and placed in a prison camp.[148] She was eventually released, only to witness first-hand the slaughter of her people and the violent occupation of her country. Seeing the unimaginable deaths and anguish the Japanese exacted upon her countrymen, Magdalena

---

147. Xiao Chua, "'Lioness of PHL guerilla spies' Maggie Leones to be buried with full honors," *GMA News Online*, last modified June 11th, 2016, last accessed December 27th, 2018, https://www.gmanetwork.com/news/lifestyle/content/573214/lioness-of-phl-guerilla-spies-maggie-leones-to-be-buried-with-full-honors/story/.
148. Filipino Veterans Recognition Project, "On July 4th: Remember Acts of Courage, Uncommon Valor," last modified July 15th, 2018, last accessed December 26th, 2018, https://usa.inquirer.net/13616/july-4th-remember-acts-courage-uncommon-valor.

Chapter 4. Filipina American Veterans

became a guerrilla. She headed to Manila and worked with a pocket resistance led by missionaries and leaders of the Emmanuel Cooperative Hospital in Manila to provide funding for the growing guerrilla resistance in the mountains to the north.

Magdalena and her team of resistance volunteers would soon be found out by the Imperial Japanese Army stationed in Manila. Magdalena received contact from a Lieutenant Colonel sent directly from the Australian Allied base, who, unbeknownst to her and her colleagues, was a double agent working for the Japanese. He tasked Magdalena with finding and securing the whereabouts and names of the resistance to the North in order to "help establish contact" between the Allies and the fledgling Philippine resistance.[149] While trying to accomplish this mission, the real representatives of the USAFIP-NL (United States Army Forces in the Philippines of Northern Luzon) captured Magdalena, believing *she* was the double agent.

Upon hearing the truth of her circumstances, and the capture, torture, and execution of her pocket resistance community in Manila at the hands of the Japanese, Magdalena became incensed to join the USAFIP-NL and continued her "special mission." Her main task, once inducted into the USAFIP-NL by the famous Colonel Russell W. Volckmann, was to secure communications and networks between the mountain guerrilla resistance of Northern Luzon and the American command center housing MacArthur in Australia. This mission, accord-

---

149. Chua, ibid.

ing to her Silver Star commendation, included carrying radio reports, intelligence, and smuggling medicine and supplies to the guerrilla resistance in the mountains of Northern Luzon from Manila, right under the Imperial Japanese Army's noses and through Japanese claimed territories.[150]

Magdalena's espionage missions would eventually earn her the title of "the Lioness of the Filipina Agents."[151] Her various guerrilla exploits included everything from recording the names and numbers of Japanese ships coming into the port of La Union, smuggling money, learning Japanese in order to misdirect Japanese soldiers to prevent them from attacking Filipino civilians and guerrillas, spending two years finding radio parts to establish a connection to the Allies in Australia, and destroying Japanese airplanes with strategically placed bombs. She accomplished all this and more while traveling the rugged terrain between occupied Manila and the mountain province guerrilla hideouts.[152] Her dedication and unrelenting grit fostered better coordination between the

---

150. Emil Guillermo, "Magdalena Leones Filipina WWII Silver Star Recipient, Who Aided MacArthur, Dies in California," *NBCNews.com: Asian America*, last modified July 5th, 2016, last accessed December 25th, 2018, https://www.nbcnews.com/news/asian-america/magdalena-leones-filipina-wwii-silver-star-recepient-who-aided-macarthur-n603566.
151. Tammerlin Drummond, "Filipina Silver Star Winner, Richmond Resident Magdalena Leones Dies at 95," last modified June 17th, 2016, last accessed December 26th, 2018, https://www.mercurynews.com/2016/06/17/filipina-silver-star-winner-richmond-resident-magdalena-leones-dies-at-95/.
152. Bea Pantoja, "Finding Magdalena," *Bea-Pantoja*, last accessed December 26th, 2018, http://www.bea-pantoja.com/finding-magdalena-leones/.

Chapter 4. Filipina American Veterans

resistance and the Allies in Australia—allowing for a more unified liberation front and a streamlined supply chain—and provided intelligence about the various Japanese strongholds in Luzon. Her efforts weakened the Japanese to the extent that General MacArthur was finally able to return to the Philippines.[153]

Though the war was over and Magdalena had come out of it a hero, it had thoroughly transformed her. After the war—at the age of twenty-five—Magdalena became the only Asian woman to be given the US Silver Star for her espionage fieldwork and gallantry in action during World War II. Only four other women in America's military history have been given such a badge of honor and prestige.[154] However, unlike other *pinay* Amazons of the resistance, who continued to bear arms and found positions in the new Philippine government or military, Magdalena chose a more traditional route for her future: to marry, have children, and put her espionage days behind her. Like Josefina Guerrero, Magdalena opted to immigrate to the United States with her family in 1969, settle in California, and take on a career as a clerk for Pacific Bell. Like Guerrero, Magdalena rarely spoke of her past life as a resistance fighter and intelligence officer for the USAFIP-NL. Her own children and grandchildren were kept in the dark much of their lives regarding their mother's exciting, yet brief, time as a crucial underground agent of the resistance.

---

153. Guillermo, ibid.
154. Leonardo Q. Nuval, *Remember Them Kindly: Some Filipinos During World War II,* Claretian Publications, 1996, pp. 31-33.

Magdalena, who transformed from a nun-in-training into a resistance fighter, and then later into a humble wife, mother, grandmother, and first-generation Filipina American, would finally be officially recognized for her courage and sacrifices as a true American citizen and veteran of World War II in 2009.[155] Under Obama's 2009 Equity Pay Act, World War II Filipino guerrillas and scouts who applied were given a lump sum of $15,000, which Magdalena was more than qualified for. On June 16th, 2016, Magdalena Leones passed away at the age of 95. As part of the memorial services due to World War II heroines, Magdalena's body was flown to the Philippines in order to receive a full hero's welcome, burial, and send-off in full military honors at the Hero's Cemetery in Fort Bonifacio, to be with the other brave men and women who served their country.[156]

Lourdes Poblete

Lourdes Poblete was another *pinay* who was also recently acknowledged for her role as a *guerrillera* under the Equity Pay Act. Over the age of 100, Poblete could still recall every event of the war as if it were yesterday. The daughter of a Filipino-American military officer, Poblete and her siblings were raised on and around American military base environments like Fort McKinley

---

155. Guillermo, ibid.
156. Filipino Veterans Recognition Project, "On July 4th: Remember Acts of Courage, Uncommon Valor."

Chapter 4. Filipina American Veterans

Lourdes Poblete as a young girl posing with her younger sisters and her parents, photographed in the 1920s. Courtesy of Mrs. Lourdes Catig-Poblete's Personal Collection.[157]

located near Pasig City on the island of Luzon. It would be Poblete's family ties to the American military that would allow her to receive an education and a strong

---

157. Catig-Poblete, Lourdes. *Family Photograph*. 1920s. Lourdes Catig-Poblete Personal Collection, San Francisco.

grasp of the English language, which would aid her in her efforts as a Luzon guerrilla.

With the fall of Corregidor to the IJA, Poblete's father, who was still employed by the American military, was forced to endure the Bataan Death March. His absence left Poblete and her family to find various means of income for their survival. Poblete's mother would conduct small domestic industries (sewing and textile work). Poblete herself would take long treks, oftentimes by *bangka*, to gather local produce and sell whatever food supplies were left once the Japanese Army took their share of the locals' harvested goods. With over six mouths to feed in one household, Poblete and her family's subsistence living came to represent just one example of the ever-tiring daily workloads Filipino families would face in wartime as the Japanese presence drained the Philippines' economy and resources.

Poblete felt an obligation to help not only her family but her fellow countrymen. She believed that she could contribute to the liberation of her country from the Japanese armed forces and joined the guerrilla movement as a teenager under the 10th Military District's Live or Die Unit.[158] As directed by her commanding guerrilla officer, Captain Julian Alvarez, Poblete's many missions included delivering propaganda (newspapers in particular) to specific guerrilla conspirators.

---

158. Manzel Delacruz, "The Women Behind the Bataan Legacy Project," *Positively Filipino: Your Window on the Filipino Diaspora*, last modified April 5th, 2017, last accessed August 5th, 2017, http://www.positivelyfilipino.com/magazine/the-women-behind-the-bataan-legacy-project.

Poblete, like other guerrilla insurgents, had to constantly remain wary of those around her. She made sure not to provide any hints of her whereabouts or affiliations, and was keen on conversing only with those who made sure to say specific code words or statements that would ensure their conversation was guerrilla organized. Poblete's experience as a guerrilla courier reveals the intense means that insurgents practiced to ensure their security and the safety of those they were involved with. Guerrillas had to be especially cautious because of the many Filipino civilians who were pro-Japanese who could have given, and in many cases, regularly did give the locations of Filipino guerrillas to Japanese intelligence so as to prove their own loyalty while securing their own safety and wellbeing under Japanese occupation.

The para-military pro-Japanese group, the *Makapili*, was one such group that believed that the Allies' defeat by the Japanese served as a stepping stone toward the Philippines' independence.[159] Filipino spies for the Japanese could easily pose as guerrilla recruits and often tried to join the resistance as fresh recruits in order to provide Japanese intelligence with information regarding guerrilla networks. Filipino guerrillas and American soldiers therefore had to provide means of evidence that proved their loyalty to the cause of liberating the Philippines when sending information to one another. American-made goods (Lucky Strike cigarettes) and propagan-

---

159. Mercedes G. Planta, "*Sakdalistas' Struggle for Philippine Independence, 1930-1945, Review*," *Philippine Studies: Historical and Ethnographic Viewpoints* Vol. 63, No. 4 (December 2014), pp. 592-593.

dist supply items that were trademarked by MacArthur (cigarette boxes, newspapers, chocolate, pencils, gum, etc.) with his slogan "I Shall Return" were the goods that guerrillas gave one another to prove their affiliation to the resistance was real.[160] Poblete's propaganda guerrilla missions which included sending coded messages hidden in newspapers, gum, or cigarette boxes confirm these historical observations as to the discrete operations of the Philippine guerrillas.

Other tasks given to Poblete included taking on specific jobs assigned to her by her guerrilla liaison, Captain Julian Alvarez. One such job included operating as a regular factory worker for a Japanese manned shipping and distributing company in the Manila region. Her covert mission was to provide reconnaissance about the details of the Japanese workhouses in the Philippines to her guerrilla commander. The job was very strenuous, forcing her to work long hours lifting shipments. The Japanese managers and overseers were very strict according to Poblete and the workers were told not to talk to other Filipino workers in the facility otherwise they would be forced to stand outside in the hot sun for the rest of the day alone.

Poblete's father was able to make it back home after the Bataan Death March around the same time that Poblete began her espionage work. One night when the

---

160. Supreme Commander of the Allied Powers, General Staff of General MacArthur, *Reports of General MacArthur: The Campaigns of MacArthur in the Pacific, Vol. I.*, Library of Congress, 1966, 81, and Bruce Henderson, *Rescue at Los Banos: The Most Daring Prison Camp Raid of World War II*, New York: HarperCollins, 2015, p. 178.

Chapter 4. Filipina American Veterans

whole family was home, Japanese officers arrived at their door asking for Poblete to come with them for questioning. Poblete had been found out for her ties to the guerrilla movement. Her father, having dealt with the Japanese during the Bataan Death March, knew that provoking them and resisting their requests would hurt the rest of their household, which included Poblete's younger siblings. Poblete's mother was distraught, shaken, and feared for the lives of all their children, but worried especially that her eldest daughter would be raped and murdered by the Japanese if she were to let her daughter go with the Japanese officers that night. Poblete's father decided with a heavy heart that Lourdes had no choice but to go with the armed men. The soldiers at the front steps of the Catig household stated that the young Lourdes would return the next day.

> "Tomorrow," according to Mrs. Poblete, "became two years."[161]

Poblete was moved to the infamous Fort Santiago where many suffering POWs and insurgents were held and killed. In the tunnels of the fort, Poblete would find a kindred spirit in her cell, another fellow *guerrillera* Filipina by the name of Natividad, or "Naty" for short. The stench of the sick and suffering Allied POWs would fill the tunnels and reminded the two young women of how desperate and terrifying their situation was. The medical

---

161. Lourdes Catig-Poblete, interview by Stacey Anne Baterina Salinas, San Francisco, July 4th, 2017.

aid afforded the captured POWs and guerrilla insurgents was little to none. Poblete remarked that "body lice were a common pain" and would line and infest her clothing and nether regions making her chores and simple movements constantly uncomfortable.[162] Showers and baths were rare and a comfortable place to relieve oneself was simply wishful thinking.

Poblete described that her main task with her cellmate was to maintain the cleanliness of the tunnels and to make blackout curtains in preparation for American bombardments of the towns surrounding Manila. The next few years were filled with desperate longings for home. Poblete worried constantly that her family might have perished after her abduction, that perhaps the Allies would never liberate the Philippines. Another thought that haunted her was the possibility that she would be forced to become a comfort woman. She contemplated daily whether or not she would be tortured or killed. The Japanese colonel in charge of the fort made sure that the "cleaning ladies" would not be harmed or sexually assaulted by ordering the Japanese soldiers not to harm the women otherwise they would be "decapitated as punishment."[163]

As the war raged on and the success of the collaborations between the guerrillas and the Allied forces changed the tide of war to benefit the Allies, Japanese officials at Fort Santiago decided to move the POWs and remaining supplies elsewhere to avoid Allied aerial

---

162. Ibid.
163. Ibid.

Chapter 4. Filipina American Veterans

bombings. Poblete and her cellmate were relocated to an old mansion belonging to one of the prominent old families of Manila, the Aranetas. Placed in the servants' quarters, Poblete and her friend felt blessed to have a restroom, shower, clean running water, and proper beds. However, the fear of aerial bombings, raids, friendly fire, and perhaps last-minute executions of POWs by fleeing Japanese soldiers ran through the minds of Poblete and her guerrilla comrade.

Confined to one room in the large mansion, escape did seem a possibility for Poblete. After a few days, the mansion became quiet and was eventually deserted. Poblete and her friend braved the empty halls of the mansion and walked out of the iron gates of the property without a scratch. The two parted ways wishing each other luck and safe travels as they walked from Manila to their neighboring hometowns, Pasig and Pasay.

> "My one regret," described Mrs. Poblete, "was that I did not look for her [Naty] after the war."[164]

Poblete's one-day trek to her hometown proved to be a frightening final stretch towards her freedom. She feared that contact with any stranger, whom she believed could be a *Makapili*, along the road would have terrible repercussions if it became known where she had come from and why. Eventually, Poblete would make it to her home, to find her family alive. The only missing smiling

---
164. Ibid.

face she was expecting to see was that of her younger brother, Ramon, who was abducted by the Japanese Army at the age of 16 and never heard from again.

> "That was the loneliest day, I loved my brother. My father said to imagine and pray that he was sent to another province, or escaped, or was let go and was being taken care of by other Filipino families who might have taken him in. He will come back."[165]
>
> —Lourdes Catig-Poblete

Poblete would lose another younger sibling once the American aerial bombings increased throughout the region of Manila and its neighboring towns. While en route with the rest of the family as they tried to find a secure place to hide, Poblete's younger sister was hit by friendly fire as they made their way through the cemeteries. Poblete tearfully recounted the thoughts that tore at her when her sister suddenly passed, "This is too much for me! Not two of my siblings. Lord, why not me instead? Not my sister."[166] It was only after the war that many Filipinos found out that the cemeteries, which many believed to be safe zones for Filipino families to hide in, were viewed by American intelligence as opportune places for fleeing IJA officers to hide in, and thus many American pilots were ordered to bomb Philippine cemeteries.

---

165. Ibid.
166. Ibid.

Chapter 4. Filipina American Veterans

As the guerrillas and Allies became more certain that the liberation of the Philippines was within reach, Poblete again offered her skills to the war effort in helping the surviving American and Filipino soldiers recover. Before the war, Poblete studied to become a nurse. Near the conclusion of the war, Poblete worked for the Red Cross for six months and would recruit her high school friends from her hometown to help jumpstart the morale of the war-weary men. Such tasks included playing the piano for them, helping soldiers write letters to be sent home, combing their hair, or providing them with basic medical care. Poblete and her peers also helped prepare veterans for their journeys back home, making sure their paperwork and itinerary were set, once they recovered from their ailments.

After the war, Poblete would serve as a secretary to Colonel Mitchum in an army hospital while attending courses at the University of Manila. There, she would also be asked to help in the beginning stages of the war crime trials of the Pacific led by General MacArthur by providing her testimonies as a guerrilla and POW. Poblete was asked to confirm the face of major Japanese officers like Colonel Nakahama, who had spared her and Naty from sexual abuse at the hands of the Japanese soldiers stationed at Fort Santiago. Poblete felt torn in helping accuse Colonel Nakahama of wartime crimes as he had shielded both her and Naty from sexual abuse but nonetheless saw it fit she submit her testimony in order to provide justice to the many Philippine families and comrades who suffered under Japanese occupation. During her time in Manila, helping with the tribunal proceedings and attending to her own work, Poblete would meet her husband, a young news reporter by the family name of Poblete, whose name she would take. Lourdes remembered fondly when Mr. Augusto Alemani Poblete interviewed her on her experiences of the war and how he "became absolutely smitten" with her in the process. Poblete married her husband and happily settled down and had her own family.

After her husband's death, Mrs. Poblete immigrated to the United States and worked at San Francisco General Hospital as a medical worker. Despite her contributions to the underground resistance, like many other guerrilla men and women, she would not be honored for her duties as a guerrilla until 2017. And like so many other *pinay guerrillas*, she also chose to travel across the Pacific to live a humble life as a medical aide in California. Her bravery and sacrifice of course did not go unnoticed. By the acknowledgment of the California State Legislature following President Barack Obama's Filipino Veterans of World War II Congressional Gold Medal Act, Filipino and Filipina guerrilla veterans like Poblete, were finally recognized for their valor. On April 8th, 2017, a strong and spirited Mrs. Lourdes Catig-Poblete well into her nineties, humbly and proudly received her long-overdue Congressional Gold Medal.

Chapter 4. Filipina American Veterans

Serapia Estojero Aremas

Samar *guerrillera* Sherry (Serapia) Aremas at the age of 26 on her college graduation day, wearing her own design and take on the traditional *mestiza* dress. In the following weeks from her graduation from Manila's Fashion School, Sherry would embark on a cargo ship towards her new life in Salinas with her husband Ricardo Aremas, both as World War II veterans, circa 1946. Courtesy of the Aremas Family Personal Collection.

Serapia Aremas was a college student when Pearl Harbor was set aflame by the Japanese. Tension and anxiety in the Pacific had been growing for quite some years, but with American military bases stationed throughout the archipelago, and the buildup and training of Filipino recruits over the last several years, Philippine citizens were optimistic about the safety and security of their country. Unfortunately, the sirens and blaring announcements at Serapia's university requesting students to leave campus and return home in the early months of 1942 signified the end of normalcy and the start of the war. Rather than go home to her barrio near Tacloban, Serapia was recruited by the local guerrilla resistance, after which she acted as a maid for a prominent local family that was loyal to the Allied front and funded operations against Japanese forces under the

Serapia's official papers as a guerrilla woman, undercover, for the Philippine Guerrilla Forces at Samar, under the commander and chief of the Northern Leyte Branch, Jose C. Santos, circa 1943. Courtesy of Aremas Family Personal Collection.

command of Lieutenant General Shiro Makino, who had recently laid siege to Serapia's home island of Leyte.

Unfortunately, the Imperial Japanese Army's (IJA) intelligence bureau soon found out about Serapia's host family and their connections.

> "The villagers said that their heads had been cut off. Their bodies were floating in the river. I left [my post] and went home to my family."

When asked how long she went into hiding from the IJA near Tacloban, Serapia responded that she was "[n]ot

Chapter 4. Filipina American Veterans

really hiding from them. We were living in a little [remote] barrio. My father made a little house and managed a little farm, along the river, close to town. A road was close enough to our homes that we [the villagers] could signal to each other using the sounds [*Serapia proceeds to knock on the table*] of the bamboo [posts] when they would see some Japanese. When you hear that sound [*she knocks again*] you and the people who lived on that road, had to go away from that road. The people who did the signal were officers [guerrillas]. A husband and wife [who were guerrillas] on that road were killed. They [the Japanese] made a hole and put the husband and wife in there, buried alive."

She continued to support the war effort by volunteering for the USAFFE once MacArthur's forces secured their position after the Battle of Leyte. As a volunteer clerk, Serapia oversaw, packaged, and delivered supplies to local Filipino families on Leyte. It was here where she met her future husband, a Filipino supply sergeant from the United States named Ricardo Aremas who was also assigned to the Allied supply warehouse. Serapia's daily duties included checking up on visiting families in need and reading through their applications for medical supplies and food rations.

Serapia recalled with fondness the simple gestures and passing signs of affection her future husband of over seventy years made towards her at the Army office building: "I would be writing at an office desk in a warehouse... I would look at him and he would look at me. I would go home, and he [future husband] would give me a package [USAFFE rations]. He wasn't allowed to do that, to give those away, but he would do that to make us [get] to know each other. Soon, he asked my mother's permission to marry me and we got married in my little town."[167]

---

167. Sherry Aremas (World War II Philippine Guerrilla, Salinas *manang* pre-1965 generation), interviewed by Stacey Salinas, April 2018.

Chapter 4. Filipina American Veterans

Photographed above are a sample of the types of food rations that Philippine volunteers like Serapia would organize and hand to war-ravaged families in Leyte.[168]

Within months of getting to know one another, the migrant farm worker turned Supply Sergeant, and the *guerrillera* turned military clerk, were married on December 3rd, 1945, four months after the Japanese were defeated in the Philippines Campaign. Later, Ricardo would help fund Serapia's endeavors as a licensed fashion designer and seamstress at Samson's Fashion College of Manila. He did this while also putting together his and his wife's papers to leave for the United States,

---

168. Tessie Jayme, "Red Cross In Manila," *Black Clouds In Manila*, last modified March 2014, last accessed December 28th, 2018, http://blackcloudsinmanila.com/Red-Cross.php.

USAFFE aides like Serapia organized, delivered, and managed the paperwork regarding the food and medical supplies. The photograph of Filipina nurses and volunteers for the Red Cross above shows the contributions of Filipina nurses and assistants packaging supplies and comfort items, also known as "ditty bags," for Allied soldiers towards the tail end of the war, circa 1945.[169]

finding a new job to support his new family, and collecting enough capital to settle in California.

After graduation, Serapia and her husband were reunited. Together they took the daring voyage to the United States aboard the USS Meigs, a vessel once used

---

169. Ibid.

Chapter 4. Filipina American Veterans

Serapia and Ricardo pose for their marriage license, circa 1945. Courtesy of the Aremas Family.

as a transfer ship for troops during the war. Serapia's husband had served in the USAFFE and thus, under the Nationality Act of 1940, which allowed Filipinos who served in American uniform to become U.S. citizens, his citizenship status changed from "alien" to naturalized Filipino American.[170] His citizenship status helped

---

170. Truman would abruptly deny the naturalization of many Filipino guerrillas, scouts, and those in both the regular and irregular units through

Serapia remain united with her husband and seek a new life abroad. Through the ratification of the War Brides Act of 1947, 118,000 Filipina/o spouses and children, including Serapia, would be able to travel with their spouses or family to the United States and become naturalized American citizens.[171]

The happy couple settled in Salinas, California, a major agrarian hub for Filipino immigrant labor since the 1920s. They had a modest start, establishing their first home within Salinas' farming labor camps by 1947. Ricardo continued to labor in the lettuce fields as an irrigation expert for three years before going to work at Fort Ord. Serapia used her degree as a professional seamstress, sewing traditional Filipiniana gowns for the local Filipina wives and families in the area for special Filipino occasions and get-togethers, along with fulfilling other miscellaneous requests from the Filipino American community. Serapia's fervent and driven personality that helped her through the war also helped her to become a successful jack-of-all-trades career woman in Salinas. During the early years of their marriage, Serapia would support their little house and home they shared with other migrant labor farming families in the labor camps

---

the Veterans Rescission Acts of 1946. The discussion of compensation and follow up on honoring the sacrifices of all Filipino World War II veterans and granting them previous promises of American citizenship in 1990, and again in 2009. Deenesh Sohoni & Amin Vafa, "The Fight to Be American: Military Naturalization, and Asian Citizenship," *Asian American Law Journal*, Vol. 17 Article 4 (January 2010): p. 146.

171. Ronald H. Bayor, *Multicultural America: An Encyclopedia of the Newest Americans,* Santa Barbara: ABC-CLIO LLC., 2011, p. 714.

Chapter 4. Filipina American Veterans

of Salinas via her various incomes. Although Serapia would come to define her status as a housewife, she continued to utilize and hire out many of her other skills. She became a professional cake decorator and beautician, with certificates for all her credentials to boot.

Serapia, upon arriving in the United States, began going by the name "Sherry." This was a split-second change suggested by her husband-to-be (Serapia, he determined, might be too difficult for Americans to pronounce let alone write) at the Army office that settled the legal work of their marriage. She also volunteered for the Filipino Women's Club of Salinas (one of the oldest Filipino American organizations established in 1930), serving as an essential dress designer and seamstress of traditional women's wear for women's benefits, galas, and fundraising events.

Serapia's new life in the United States was symbolized by a multitude of roles, risky economic ventures, and cultural change. Nevertheless, she met those challenges head-on, and in the process, raised a young family, cultivated the Filipino American and Asian American communities of the Central Coast through her volunteer and auxiliary work, and became a woman representative of a new postwar age: a first-generation Asian American woman with a multifaceted professional persona, a community influencer, and an ever-multitasking mother and homemaker with a courageous World War II veteran *guerrillera* background.

In October of 2021, Serapia passed away at the age of 102. Until her last days, Serapia continued to support her Filipino American community as one of the oldest members of the Filipino Women's Club. Both she and her daughter, Susan Aremas (a devoted and retired school teacher), continued to lead community projects and helped to oversee scholarship fundraisers for their local Filipina/o/x American Salinas youths. Serapia, also known by her community and family as "Lola Sherry," left an incredible mark in Fil-Am history as a *pinay* trailblazer in more ways than one.

Lourdes Evangelista-Castro

Even after the war, Filipina American veterans who arrived in the United States, like Serapia, remained driven in their endeavors to protect the interests and heritage of their ethnic communities. Lourdes Evangelista-Castro was also one such neighbor and community leader who found herself aggrandized by her *guerrillera* personality to continue serving her Fil-Am neighborhood and fellow veterans. Like Serapia who volunteered for Filipina/o-led neighborhood organizations, Lourdes also volunteered in San Jose's Fil-am hub, particularly at the Filipino Siquig Northside Community Center. There she preserved Filipino-American culture and helped to maintain an inviting and warm environment for first and second-generation Asian American families in the San Jose area. Evidence of Lourdes' impact is in how she is fondly remembered by her community and family. Her daughter, Marisa Otto, described her "as a highly devoted

Chapter 4. Filipina American Veterans

Photographed above is Lourdes Castro, who at the age of eighteen served as a frontline responder and medic.[172]

mother and a grandmother and she was a trailblazer."[173] Other veterans who worked with her such as Nolasco Mapalad described her as "very cooperative... helpful to her colleagues in explaining page by page veteran's benefits."[174] Such acts of commitment in protecting and

---

172. Ben Menor & Marissa Castro Otto, "Lourdes Castro: The Story of a Rare and Great Hero," *Inquirer.Net*, last modified December 14th, 2011, last accessed December 19th, 2018, https://globalnation.inquirer.net/20861/lourdes-castro-1926-2011-the-story-of-a-rare-and-great-hero.
173. Henni Espinosa, "Pinay War Veteran Dies Fighting for Justice," *ABS-CBN.News*, last modified December 28th, 2011, last accessed December 26th, 2018, https://news.abs-cbn.com/global-filipino/12/27/11/pinay-war-veteran-dies-fighting-justice.
174. Ibid.

invigorating the collectivity of one's hometown signal a common trait found among humble veteran heroes such as Serapia and Lourdes.

Lourdes' post-war community-building career was just as rich and impactful as her time as a guerrilla. At the age of eighteen, Lourdes Evangelista-Castro was inducted into the US Army for her bravery and courage in undermining the Japanese and rescuing Filipino and American soldiers on the front lines. Lourdes brought multiple skill sets essential to war to the liberation front, being an experienced first responder medic, intelligence courier, and soldier.[175] As a guerrilla working for the Philippine Commonwealth Army and its Medical Corps, Lourdes pulled injured American and Filipino soldiers out of harm's way to tend to their wounds and participated in the famous liberation of the POW concentration camp of Los Banos. Due to her valiant efforts, she was inducted into the US Army; one of only two Filipinas during the war to officially be granted that honor.

After the war, Lourdes continued pursuing her passion for medicine. She would go on to receive both a bachelor's and master's degree in pharmacy, eventually working as a pharmacist at Fort Bonifacio (formerly known as Fort McKinley), what is now the headquarters of the Philippine Army in Metro Manila. Lourdes would marry, raise a family, build and run her own

---

175. Ysa Singson, "4 Empowering Pinay Warriors You Should Know: Not Your Stereotypical Maria Clara," *Cosmopolitan.ph*, last modified September 11th, 2016, last accessed December 23rd, 2018, https://www.cosmo.ph/lifestyle/empowering-pinay-warriors-filipiknow-a00177-20160912.

Chapter 4. Filipina American Veterans

pharmacy business, and eventually become president of the Nueva Ecija Pharmaceutical Association.

In 1986, Lourdes and her family immigrated and settled in San Jose, California. It was there that she reclaimed her vigor and passion as a *guerrillera:* pursuing the reinstatement of all Filipina/o World War II veterans' benefits and their rights as neglected war heroes. Lourdes was one of the fortunate few who did receive full benefits, including a pension granted to war veterans. Just as she did as a wartime guerilla, Lourdes continued to look out for her fellow Filipina/o comrades who served. She spoke on behalf of Filipina/o veterans as a council member who served on the Filipino American Community Development Council Inc. and became a founding member of the American Legion Northside Post 858, based in San Jose, where most of the members were Filipino veterans.[176]

On December 3rd, 2011, Lourdes passed away at the age of 85. Her legacy and historical narrative portray her as a hardworking woman of many talents and skills. Indeed, she was a pharmacist, businesswoman, community organizer and leader, civil rights activist, and World War II veteran. Her largest contribution to her countrymen and women—re-opening the conversation of Filipinos' veterans' status and recognition—continues to be an uphill battle. The lack of Asian ethnic groups' inclusion in World War II narratives marks the inherent racial, postcolonial, and political biases found in mainstream western and world histories of the war.

---

176. Espinosa, ibid.

Stories like Lourdes' are difficult to locate and bring to the surface, particularly because narratives like hers are remembered only by their own families and communities. Despite these obstacles restricting the broader recognition for women like Lourdes, her accomplishments continue to expand the breadth and scope of immigrant and labor history to include transnational women of color veterans.

Pinay guerrilleras' actions and stations, regardless of how they understood their positions in the resistance, served as the seedlings that allowed for the underground resistance to carry on and find hope. Even for those hands who had little to no socio-economic means of political power—as Filipina women did before, during, and after the war—their experiences and contributions still provided lay people with the hope that one's limited station held merit and a means for more. These women lived very private lives, never speaking of their wartime exploits, focusing their postwar energies instead on supporting and raising their families. Although their wartime achievements displayed heroism that challenged gender conventions, many of these women found their future narratives bound yet again to serve their families. As a consequence, their *pinay* heroic experiences became subsumed by their humble dedication to their families, and thus, their stories were rarely acknowledged or discussed until recently.

One of President Barack Obama's goals during his presidency was to "right" long-overdue obligations to

Chapter 4. Filipina American Veterans

historically marginalized peoples both on a domestic and international scale. For example, the American Recovery and Reinvestment Act of 2009 created the World War II Filipino Veterans Equity Compensation Fund. This fund represented a lump-sum payment to eligible Filipino World War II veterans. President Obama's White House Initiative on AAPIs (Asian American Pacific Islanders) worked with Filipino veterans to allow for fair, efficient processing, and review of applications to fund awards to as many veterans as possible. As of 2016, a total of 42,755 applications were processed with over $225 million having been paid out.[177]

The World War II Filipino Veterans Equity Compensation Fund represents one of the first steps toward recognizing and including Filipina/o contributions to both American history and World War II narratives. The *guerrillera* veterans covered in this chapter point to the many gaps in such popular histories. These women's immigrant histories may appear, at first glance, to be isolated and only mentioned by the communities they lived and served in. However, in reality, their compassion and dedication to serve their families and local communities in quieter capacities—towards what others might consider less extraordinary ends—reveal how their days as *guerrilleras* granted them a certain kind of resilience. These "ordinary" women created new lives in

---

177. Billy Dec, "Honoring Filipino WWII Veterans this Filipino American History Month," *The White House: President Barack Obama*, last modified October 3rd, 2016, last accessed December 24th, 2018, https://obamawhitehouse.archives.gov/blog/2016/10/03/honoring-filipino-wwii-veterans-filipino-american-history-month.

the United States, focused on their families, and aimed for careers that supported a simple, self-effacing livelihood for themselves, their families, and their own Asian American communities. Their selflessness and devotion to such "modest" priorities and ability to persevere in any environment or career they chose, taken together with their exceptional wartime feats, reveal that they too are heroes, despite humble appearances.

Chapter 5

The Legacy of the Asian Woman Soldier

MacArthur's famous landing on the island of Leyte in October of 1944 launched another wave of guerrilla warfare that forced the surrender of the Imperial Japanese Army. The Battle of Manila began in February of 1945 and would continue for a month, causing many Allied, Japanese and civilian casualties in the capital.[178] After the American and Philippine troops reclaimed Manila, MacArthur deemed the Philippines liberated, leaving the final task of eliminating the last stands of Japanese resistance to the guerrillas. Huk commanders like Simeona Punsalan and Liwayway were tasked with rooting out the last of the Japanese stragglers in Central Luzon. The fighting between the remaining individual enemy units and Philippine guerrilla troops continued until the Japanese branch in the mountain region of Northern Luzon officially surrendered in August 1945.

For most resistance fighters the end of the Japanese occupation marked the end of their guerrilla career. Some continued to fight against the new Philippine

---

178. James M. Scott, *Rampage: MacArthur, Yamashita, and the Battle of Manila,* W.W. Norton & Company, 2018, Part II, Chapter 6.

government, which in many ways continued the landed bureaucracies and social caste systems previously implemented by both the Spanish and American occupations. Huk women like Simeona Punsalan, Liwayway, and Mariano-Pomeroy would go underground with their husbands, fighting for the rights and inclusion of peasant farmers, the landless laborers, and those Filipinas/os denied veterans' benefits. In contrast, other guerrillas considered their mission accomplished when the Japanese signed their official surrender in 1945.

Public Memory and Remembering the Filipina War Hero

The Philippine Resistance reflected the cultural and socio-economic diversity of the Philippine Islands. From socialist peasant farmers, indigenous recruits, Chinese-Filipino union workers, middle-school teachers, ROTC youths, to Moro (Philippine Muslim) warriors, the range and inclusivity of the men and women who participated in the struggle against the Japanese Imperial Army was incredible.[179] The women guerrilla fighters especially made major contributions to the liberation of the Philippines, but unfortunately, as with other ethnic minority guerrilla fighters, have received less acknowl-

---

179. Chinese-Filipino labor union workers in Manila formed their own guerrilla unit, Wha Chi, also known as Squadron 48. Fannie Tan Koa, "The Wha Chi Guerrillas," *The Philippine Star*, last modified May 24th, 2015, last accessed November 14, 2021, https://www.pressreader.com/philippines/the-philippine-star/20150524/283536564341187.

Chapter 5. The Legacy of the Asian Woman Soldier

edgment and discussion in World War II histories of the Pacific Theater.

During the early half of the twentieth century, the Philippines witnessed few advances in women's rights. However, with the threat of war and the encroachment of the Japanese Imperial Army upon the Philippine Islands, the patriarchal and religiously conservative culture of the Philippines could not afford to maintain its traditional gender hierarchy. The grassroots resistance drew in the patriotic fervor of many Filipinas, who saw the guerrilla resistance as an opportunity to liberate their homeland as well as prove the "capabilities of their sex." Their guerrilla efforts proved women were more than capable of taking on numerous roles: soldiers, leaders, activists, journalists, nurses, doctors, spies, and dedicated patriots. Filipina guerrillas proved to be a vital aspect of both soldiering and reconnaissance missions, allowing for the Allies to gain the opportunity to retake the Philippines.

Historians estimate that, for every ten male guerrillas, one Filipina guerrilla served in the underground resistance.[180] Over 260,000 male Filipino guerrillas served the resistance effort.[181] The fact that only male guerrillas have been counted reflects how Filipinas in wartime history have been neglected, either being ignored or not counted as officially serving, despite female guer-

---

180. Lanzona, *Amazons of the Huk Rebellion*, p. 7.
181. Nicholas Trajano Molnar, *American Mestizos, The Philippines, and the Malleability of Race: 1898-1961*, University of Missouri Press, 2017, p. 126.

rilla populations representing possibly more than 10% of the guerrilla resistance. These statistics, along with the very few surviving resources about Filipina guerrilla efforts, bring to light the missing narratives of a traditionally American-centered history of the liberation of the Philippines in World War II. The wartime experiences of women of color in the Pacific highlight the various contributions, struggles, and cultural diversity that aided and represented the Allied front in the Pacific.

Filipina *guerrilleras*, like their male peers, were aware of the risks and sacrifices they made in their efforts to push the Japanese Imperial Army out of the Philippines. One of the added fears and risks that all Filipinas shared, which their male peers did not, was the threat of rape and being forcibly used as comfort women (sex slaves) for the Japanese Imperial Army. Despite the risks of death, torture, and rape, the Filipina *guerrilleras* of the Philippine Resistance persevered, representing the hardy and selfless cause of both the liberation from the Japanese imperial regime and progress toward women's rights in Southeast Asia.

The invasion and occupation of the Philippines by the Japanese Imperial Army would breed another generation of Filipina *guerrilleras*, armed with both nationalist determination and soldierly stamina. The Allied surrender at Corregidor, the horrors of the Bataan Death March, and the Philippines' long history of female fighters culminated in leadership opportunities for empowered *pinays*,

Chapter 5. The Legacy of the Asian Woman Soldier

primarily because of their staunch resistance to enemy occupation throughout the duration of the war. Unfortunately, despite the efforts and sacrifices of *pinay guerrilleras*, Asian women's roles in the war continue to be commonly depicted within the framework of traditional gender conventions: as nurses, caregivers, and motherly hands and faces lending their shoulder to the wounded allies. These portrayals of *guerrilleras*, rather than their efforts as leaders, fighters, and scouts, are far more prevalent in both the written histories and material culture produced during and after the war. Nevertheless, as this book demonstrates, the roles of *pinay* insurgents were far more active and diverse than what American and Filipino films, wartime literature, and propaganda material have promoted over the last seventy-five years.

Popular movies released after the war portrayed Filipina women in the background as supporting roles. In both Filipino and American cinema, Filipinas were portrayed as either "exotic" love interests to the main characters, nurses, village non-combatants, or as bystanders. In films such as *An American Guerrilla in the Philippines*, released in 1950, the hero and leader of the resistance is an American soldier, Ensign Chuck Palmer, stranded in the Philippines following the Japanese invasion. He falls in love with a rich French woman married to a Filipino landowner who later in the film becomes a guerrilla. Women resistance sympathizers portrayed in this film are seen as far more interested in love than war. Even worse, the film does not recognize Filipina/o actors in the credits, with the main "Filipino" protagonists not being ethnically Filipino; the role of the Filipino landowner was played by Spanish actor, Juan Torena, while the Leyte Filipino resistance fighter was played by American actor Tommy Cooke.[182] In the film, the Western Allies are front and center as the leaders and heroes of the resistance, not Filipinos, and certainly not Filipinas.

In the movie poster shown above, the Filipina actress who is not credited in the film, is seen as a silent villager, a pseudo-medical aide, whose role falls into the part of the broad Philippine landscape. She is a villager, a nurse, but not one who is deemed essential or part of the resistance on a militant level.[183]

Postwar Filipino films were also guilty of portraying Filipinas in war as lovesick heroines, secondary to

---

182. IMDB, "Actor: Juan Torena," *IMDB.com*, last accessed December 27th, 2018, https://www.imdb.com/name/nm0867944/.
183. IMDB, "American Guerrilla In the Philippines," *IMDB.com*, https://www.imdb.com/title/tt0042195/?ref_=ttfc_fc_tt.

the male protagonists. Film scholars have dubbed the late 1940s for Filipino cinema as the "Liberation" period.[184] These wartime films highlight the struggles of Filipinos, particularly as noble heroes of the resistance. Two films that capture the inclusion of women guerrillas are *Batalyon XIII* (1949) and *Guerilyera* (1946). In both films, *mestiza* actress Carmen Rosales takes center stage. She herself was a *guerrilla* who on numerous occasions disguised herself as a man to avoid Japanese suspicion. She was a spy and sharpshooter guerrilla, driven by the murder of her husband by the Japanese at the start of the war.[185] In these films, she plays a guerrilla fighter, modeled after her own experiences. She brandishes guns, has a bright and spunky personality, and is filmed in a way that does not subordinate her to her male comrades. Alas, she too was a woman who gave into more romantic desires, being portrayed as a supportive lover as much as she was a soldier.

Rosales' films during the "Liberation" era reflect the earliest public memories and sentiments about female guerrillas during the war. Although Rosales portrayed women fighters as independent, adept with weapons, and qualified in strategizing and espionage, her characters were still susceptible to more "feminine" virtues,

---

184. Danny Dolor, "Carmen Rosales as Guerilyera," last modified June 14th, 2014, last accessed December 27th, 2018, https://www.pressreader.com/philippines/the-philippine-star/20150614/282402693010462.

185. Marichu Maceda, "Carmen Rosales: The Genuine Superstar," *PhilStar Global*, last modified March 6th, 2005, last accessed December 27th, 2018, https://www.philstar.com/entertainment/2005/03/06/269261/carmen-rosales-genuine-superstar.

Sampaguita Pictures movie posters of *Guerilyera* (1946) starring a *guerrillera* herself, Carmen Rosales as the main actor and protagonist.[186]

with her films highlighting her *mestiza* beauty and her love interests.

Another Filipino film, *Victory Joe* (1946), also hails from the same "Liberation" cinema era that leaves a rather bland portrayal of Filipinas affected by the war. *Mestiza* actress Norma Blancaflor plays the role of a country girl named Rosie mourning the loss of her soldier boyfriend who, early in the film, is believed to have died in battle. She soon becomes the object of affection of an American soldier, played by Art Cantrell. Despite

---

186. Video 48, "Carmen Rosales," *Video 48: A Virtual Online Library and Archive On Philippine Cinema*, last modified April 30th 2008, last accessed December 27th, 2018, http://video48.blogspot.com/search?q=Carmen+Rosales. Danny Dolor, "Carmen Rosales as Guerilyera," last modified June 14th, 2014, last accessed December 27th, 2018, https://www.pressreader.com/philippines/the-philippine-star/20150614/282402693010462.

Chapter 5. The Legacy of the Asian Woman Soldier

the stigma attached to Filipinas who entertained or dated American officers, typically seen as women with "loose" morals, Rosie returns the officer's affections thinking that this new romance will help her to overcome the loss of her previous lover. As the war comes to a close and the American troops receive their discharge papers to return to the United States, Rosie is torn up emotionally yet again as her Filipino soldier, played by Rogelio De La Rosa, surprisingly returns hoping to start afresh with Rosie in the countryside.

Scene from *Victory Joe*, 1946. The main actress in nearly every scene is accompanied by her male love interest, thus rarely giving her character the opportunity to prioritize her needs before her romantic interests. Courtesy of Video 48 and IMDB.[187]

---

187. Directed by Manuel Silos. LVN Pictures, Metro Manila, 1946. "Victory Joe," IMDB, Poster and scene capture, last accessed November 2021, https://www.imdb.com/title/tt0442549/.

Throughout the film, Blancaflor's character, in essence, represents a woman in a war driven only by her emotions. Among the other recurrent themes associated with the afflicted war-weary Filipina that the character Rosie fulfills, another gendered motif that is most visible is how she is defined by her romantic relationships with men. Her sole role in the war, unfortunately, is as a figure of emotional support for her lovers on the front lines. It is the men in the film whose actions and decisions move the story along. Both soldiers force Rosie to make a choice between which lover she will take and it is the two soldiers in the end who jointly, and without hard feelings, decide which man is best suited for Rosie; the Filipino veteran Eduardo.[188] Rosie's personality and absent decision-making thus play into the classical interpretation of Philippine gender conventions of the period; that even under the duress of war, women such as Rosie were relegated to the roles of a civilian bystander who could only serve in the war as a supportive, doting partner.

The film production depicting Colonel Yay Panlilio's war experience and biography, *The Crucible*, played on similar tropes of Filipina femininity. The film, *Cry Freedom* (1959), starred another *mestiza* actress, Rosa Rosal, as Colonel Yay Panlilio.[189] The film portrayal of Panlilio

---

188. Rogelio De La Rosa & Norma Blancaflor, *Victory Joe*, directed by Manuel Silos. LVN Pictures, Metro Manila, 1946.
189. *Cry Freedom*, film, 1959, 93 minutes. Lamberto V. Avellana, director. Actors: Pancho Magalona, Rosa Rosal. Film Summary: A man and a woman fight for the freedom of their country—Marking with his gun —Yay with her typewriter. Thrown together by a cause greater than either of them they share the suffering of the flesh and the spirit

is also guilty of emphasizing and elevating Rosa's/Panlilio's *mestiza* attributes, and also portrayed Rosa's character, like Panlilio's wartime memoir, as more of a love interest to Colonel Agustin (played by Pancho Magalona), rather than a military *guerrillera* leader in her own right. Their love affair is central to the film, with Panlilio's character's charm and beauty being directly associated with her romantic relationship, rather than with her leadership role in Marking's guerrilla unit. In nearly every scene, Panlilio is depicted more as an attachment to the central figure of Marking's guerrilla troops, Colonel Agustin, rather than as a free-thinking woman who stood on her own as a soldier.

Within the last decade, the Obama Administration sought to challenge the conservative and gendered narrative of the Pacific Theater's guerrilla history. Indeed, the Filipino Veterans Equity Compensation Fund currently recognizes female guerrillas for their noble participation and activity—if such individuals or their family can prove their participation with the proper legal paperwork. For those women who contributed to the resistance's cause, finding the resources, time, and additional energy to put together one's papers, even after the war, was a grueling task. Many guerrillas, particularly those in more remote regions, such as the indigenous peoples such as the *Aetas,* continue to find it nearly im-

---

among the country's guerrilla fighters. They emerge, out of the crucible of war, heroes-and lovers. IMDB "Cry Freedom," *IMDB.com*, last accessed December 27th, 2018, https://www.imdb.com/title/tt0054771/plotsummary.

The 1959 Banaue Films film posters of the movie *Cry Freedom*. The subheadings and images chosen for the popular movie posters depict Panlilio as more of a romantic interest rather than a *guerrillera* at first glance.[190]

---

190. Danny Dolore, "Cry Freedom: Love & War," *Philippine Star*, last modified April 9th, 2016, last accessed December 23rd, 2018, https://www.philstar.com/entertainment/2016/04/09/1571156/cry-freedom-love-war. Video 48, "THE FIFTIES # 618: PANCHO MAGALONA AND ROSA ROSAL IN LAMBERTO V. AVELLANA'S "CRY

possible to secure proof (which requires the personal funding for lawyers to oversee their request) of their role in the war.[191]

Gendered expectations serve to further prevent *pinay guerrilleras* of any opportunity to successfully file for their benefits. If a woman served as a nurse or support staff to the guerrillas, or even housed or fed the guerrillas, does she count as an official guerrilla, even if she did not physically fight the Japanese herself? What if she was a pledged guerrilla combatant like Captain Diaz was in Yay Panlilio's memoir but the only proof that her family could rely on to apply for family veteran's benefits were scattered accounts of other soldiers' narratives? Such examples speak directly to the gendered cultural biases that women of color face, as well as their continual struggle against intersectional (gender, racial, class, nationality, citizenship, labor-based) prejudices.

The *guerrillera* generation is currently reaching their late nineties and early hundreds, and their stories will soon be forgotten if efforts to preserve their histories continue to be hindered by dominating male-centered narratives tinged with discriminative gender tones and overly broad interpretations of women's roles and agency

---

FREEDOM" (1959)," *Video48: A Virtual Online Library and Archive of Philippine Cinema*, last modified April 22nd, 2014, last accessed December 27th, 2018, http://video48.blogspot.com/2014/04/the-fifties-618-pancho-magalona-and.html.

191. Tonette Orejas, "Pension Elusive for Aeta Guerrillas," *Inquirer.Net*, last modified March 2nd, 2014, last accessed December 28th, 2018, https://newsinfo.inquirer.net/769917/pension-elusive-for-aeta-guerrillas.

throughout the war. As exemplified by *guerrilleras* such as Serapia Aremas and Lourdes Castro, women's roles on the front lines of the liberation front are evidence of female heroes re-defining the hyper-masculinized space of the Pacific Theater.

Despite *guerrillera* efforts and their experiences, many saw their roles as inconsequential, painting themselves as supporting characters, middle (wo)men simply trying to do the right thing. Or, in other case studies, like that of Serapia Aremas and Lourdes Poblete, they saw themselves merely as volunteers who intently listened and followed orders coming down from the real "center of the action," their male captains or peers. In truth, the war would transform these women, making them just as impactful as the male guerrillas and captains who led them. By stepping into the role of liberator, *guerrilleras* challenged universal gender conventions and racialized colonial hierarchies. They liberated their home barrios and their country from the Japanese occupation. Their dedication to the front lines reveals just how capable *all* Philippine citizens were of self-government and of establishing political agendas that were in their best interests.

Nevertheless, *pinay* participation in the war, unbeknownst to them, further influenced their actions and unrelenting character in the postwar era. It is true that they might have followed the traditional outlook expected of Filipinas—they married and established their own homes and future for their families. Nonetheless, these women were still taking a risk, immigrating and rearing their children in a foreign place like the United

Chapter 5. The Legacy of the Asian Woman Soldier

States during a time when xenophobia and racial prejudices were rampant. Their bravery earned them their economic independence postwar when American values reverted back to emphasizing women's roles as homemakers during the Cold War. In such an environment, even the act of wanting and pursuing an education in the United States as a full-time mother in a highly racialized environment was risky. For these former *guerrilleras*, their wartime attitude stuck with them, with their achievements going on to inspire the next generation of Filipinas and *pinays* to constantly strive to protect and ensure the futures of not only their country but of their communities both in the Philippines and abroad as well.

Conclusion

> **FILIPINO GUERRILLAS**
> By Greg. S. San Diego
>
> We did not sleep—we who refused to die,
> Nor thirbed to face war on our native ground:
> We did not weep, but stood against the cry
> Of madmen bent on spreading griefs around.
>
> We weren't afraid; fear was not in our blood.
> We only knew that freedom must be strong.
> Else all would be but worthless gifts of God
> And life, a drab and lonely thing of song.
>
> To face the common foe, to hope and wait,
> Then jump at some opportune time to kill;
> To blast the heart of madness out of hate
> And write our tale of brav'ry on the hill—
>
> We are the men who fought and waited long,
> For we believed that freedom must be strong.

A poem by a Filipino American poet, Greg San Diego, describing their patriotic zeal and dedication to the Philippines' liberation from the perspective of a guerrilla male soldier, *Philippines Mail*, circa 1945.[192]

When reading World War II narratives such as *Men of Destiny: The American and Filipino Guerrillas During the Japanese Occupation of the Philippines*, the Filipi-

---

192. Greg S. San Diego, "Filipino Guerrillas," *The Philippines Mail*, February 1945, Steinbeck Public Library, Salinas.

na guerrilla presence is blatantly absent. Despite the immense depth and variety that World War II literature and historiography offer, the people of color, particularly women of color in all theaters of the war, are glossed over. Women portrayed in wartime literature are primarily understood as passive, supporting figures, labeled as wives, cooks, couriers, and nurses for resistance fighters, or, more commonly, depicted as victims or casualties of war. The experiences of American female spies, military wives and daughters, and nurses, like those of the Angels of Bataan highlighted in Elizabeth Norman's work *We Band of Angels: The Untold Story of the American Women Trapped on Bataan*, have only recently come to light.

Norman's historical piece conveys the physical and psychological turmoil American nurses felt as they tried to make do with what little resources they had to heal both the Filipino and American soldiers under their care in the tunnels of Corregidor. After the fall of Corregidor, the American and Filipino nurses of Bataan were captured by the Imperial Japanese Army. Though they were not forced to walk the Bataan Death March, they were forced into the POW internment camps of Santo Tomas and Los Banos. The American nurses continued to help the soldiers in the camps with what little resources they were given by the Japanese, while they themselves were also under physical duress, contracting scurvy and pellagra.

The liberation of the camps in 1945 by the combined efforts of the Allied troops and Philippine guer-

Conclusion

rillas meant that the American nurses could finally go home. However, as Norman describes from the interviews conducted with twenty veteran nurses in their late eighties, the nurses were not to be given distinguished recognition for their sacrifices and courage by the American Army. Rather, upon returning home, the women were asked questions that were gender prejudiced and insensitive, regarding how they felt about contemporary fashion, or whether they were raped. In other words, they were asked nothing along the lines of their devotion to their country and profession.[193]

Norman's *We Band of Angels* (1999) and Theresa Kaminski's *Prisoners in Paradise: American Women in the Wartime South Pacific* (2000), are some of the few pieces of historical literature that investigate and add to women's history in the Pacific Theater. Kaminski's more recent book, *Angels of the Underground: The American Women Who Resisted the Japanese In the Philippines in World War II* (2016), expands the discussion of the female participants of the resistance but mainly as the title suggests, from a Euro-American women's perspective. And although Kaminski is keen to take note of the *mestiza* Filipina guerrillas or collaborators such as Yay Panlilio and Florence Ebersole, the presence, scope, and broader perspective of the Filipina guerrilla is unevenly distributed, or minimal.[194] Indeed, Norman and Kaminski's

---

193. Elizabeth M. Norman, *We Band of Angels: The Untold Story of the American Women Trapped on Bataan,* New York: Random House Trade Paperback, 2013, p. 226.
194. Theresa Kaminski, *Angels of the Underground*, p. 29, 178, 230, 341.

works provide another entry to the remarkable vanguard moments in women's world history by highlighting American women's wartime biographies. Yet, even so, the experiences of Filipina *guerrilleras*, nurses, civilians, and mothers—the women of color in the Pacific—remain scattered, voiceless, invisible, and absent.

Filipina *guerrilleras* came from all walks of life. Some were Communist Party members like Commander Liwayway, who hoped to reshape the postwar Philippines into a more egalitarian state. Others were film actresses such as Carmen Rosales, who became further incensed and galvanized to join the resistance after her husband's death at the hands of the Imperial Japanese Army. Filipina guerrilla fighters, despite their diverse backgrounds, had a common goal: to liberate their nation from Japanese occupation, secure the Philippine peoples' civil rights and independence, and restore the islands they called home. In their fight for liberation, these Filipina warriors showcased the underlying resilience and overwhelming untapped potential women of color had as military, political, and educational leaders, regardless of class, race, religion, and gender.

Guerrilleras fought on multiple fronts: against gender and racial prejudices, the Japanese occupation, and intra-ethnic gender politics. Many *guerrilleras* would never be fully recognized for their efforts in the Pacific Theater, which has perpetuated the imagery of the underground resistance as a male-dominated and hyper-masculine wartime environment. The hurdles that *guerrilleras* had to overcome to establish their own niche

Conclusion

Filipinas of the Women Auxiliary Service, Manila, circa 1941. Many Filipinas who served in WAS continued to operate as *guerrilleras* throughout the war and hid their status as WAS officers so as not to attract the attention of IJA intelligence.[195]

as soldiers and military and community leaders were directly influenced and made more insurmountable by the limitations of traditional gender and Filipino cultural norms. Filipinas found themselves delegated to the caregiver and supporting roles. Those Filipinas who sought to participate on the battlefield, or in strategic and leadership positions, were doubly questioned and challenged by male superiors who continuously tried to maintain gendered relationships of power, even in extreme wartime climates.

---

195. Eduardo de Leon, "Women Auxiliary Service, Manila, 1941," *Pinterest*, Photograph, last modified July 2021, last accessed November 2021, https://www.pinterest.com/pin/336995984618739139/.

By maintaining gender norms in camps, civilian settings, and familial households, Filipino resistance and military leaders could still hold onto one strong aspect of Filipino cultural normalities—patriarchal dominance—in the face of Japanese occupation.

The *guerrilleras* of World War II—their military leadership, espionage, love of their country, and culture—hearken back to the Filipina warrior narrative exemplified first by the mighty Princess Urduja. However, like Urduja, whose history transformed into folklore and myth, so too did the contributions and faces of the female resistance fighters of the Philippines blur into distinct and narrow categories of the preferred traditional type of heroine. Those women whose sacrifices, personalities, social caste, or appearance did not align with the cookie cutter narrative of the imagined Filipina Amazon, were re-imagined as having more supportive roles in the war. Other *guerrilleras*, who did not partake in the postwar politics of the new Philippine Republic or military have, unfortunately, been nearly forgotten. Their stories continue to fall through the cracks of recently established fields of scholarship, like women's history, world history, and immigrant labor/migration history.

The women resistance fighters in this book have, in one way or another, been affected by the gender bias that so often marginalizes the efforts of women in war. Indeed, as we have seen, many *guerrilleras* were characterized as overly emotional, romantic, and simpler compared to their male counterparts. As the biased descriptions of Yay Panlilio's contributions reveal, they supposedly gave into girlish whims and the charms of male soldiers. Other women, like the Huk commander Culala (Dayang-Dayang), was remembered as a self-involved commander who gave in too easily to selfish desires and was far too aggressive, selfish, and self-aggrandizing, leading to a terrible and shameful execution. The "ordinary" Filipina resistance soldiers, who chose to make the daring trek across the Pacific, became more defined by their career as homemakers rather than as *guerrilleras*. Like other women who were part of the second wave of Asian immigration patterns, they became known as perpetually foreign, loyal, and submissive "War Bride[s]."[196]

Filipina resistance fighters were forced to stay true to traditional forms of gender etiquette whilst operating as guerrillas. Even in extreme environments, women who wanted to participate in the war felt compelled to act as caregivers rather than fighters. Even when they did fight alongside men, they still had to act as mothers and sisters more than they would have liked to. Due to the gender hierarchy that defined the Philippines, *guerrilleras* were consistently criticized for their desire to fight, let alone be seen on the ground among men, and were even given harsh court martials and sentences for speaking out against the men they outranked, as exemplified by Commander Culala. Despite these setbacks, the Filipina guerrilla stories that survive are a remark-

---

196. Maddalena Marinari, Madeline Hsu, Maria Cristina Garcia ed., *A Nation of Immigrants Reconsidered: US Society in an Age of Restriction, 1924-1965,* University of Illinois Press, 2018, "Chapter 11: Japanese War Brides and the Normalization of Family Unification After World War II."

able testament to the women of color who defied such gendered odds and survived captivity, brutal beatings, and rape, and who continued to advocate for the recognition of Filipinas and their role in ending the Japanese occupation.

Pinay veterans could be described in a number of ways, including as confidently aggressive, soft, charismatic, quick-thinking, posh, peasant farmers, socialists, six-foot Amazons, lepers, mothers, soldiers, mixed-race, activists, and more. Whichever description is used to memorialize these women, *guerrilleras* in one way or another reshaped gender conventions on their own terms, both during the upheaval of war and the period that followed. They, along with countless other inspired Filipinas, would continue using their strength to oversee the newly independent Philippines during the Cold War. The hardy Huk women, like the lipstick-toting Commander Liwayway and Commander Simeona Punsalan, would continue the good fight for the inclusion of peasant farmers, laborers, and fair representation of Huk-communist veterans well into the late twentieth century. Others immigrated to the United States, hoping to create a new life for themselves and their families as mothers and career women. Regardless of the paths these women took in their later years, their confidence, stamina, and determination forged new opportunities and futures for women of color on a global scale.

For more information regarding the Pacific Theater, the guerrilla resistance in the Philippines, and more remarkable first-hand accounts of what life was like in the Pacific Theater, please look into the Pacific Atrocities Education's other publications:

Wantakan Nicolette Arcardo. *Siamese Sovereignty: Thailand's Strategy of Political Duality During World War II*. Pacific Atrocities Education, 2019.

Jenny Chan. *The Undrowning Lotus: A WW2 Historical Novel, Based on a True Story of a Sexual Slavery Survivor*. Pacific Atrocities Education, 2020.

Jenny Chan & Derek Pua. *Three Years, Eight Months: The Japanese Occupation of Hong Kong*. Pacific Atrocities Education, 2017.

Quin Cho and Sunwoo Park. *Competing Empires in Burma: A Chronicle of the China-Burma-India Theater of Operations in World War 2*. Pacific Atrocities Education, 2021.

Mei Mei Chun-Moy, Sally Ma, Mark Witzke. *Fall of Singapore: The Undefeatable British Fortress Conquered*. Pacific Atrocities Education, 2017.

Ally Diwik and Junyi Han. *The Forgotten Theater of WWII of China-Burma-India: The Untold Story of the First Chinese Expeditionary Force*. Pacific Atrocities Education, 2020.

Paulina Hernandez, Julie Porter, & Christopher Sayas. *Cannibalism Culture: The Bushido Horror in World War II*. Pacific Atrocities Education, 2018.

Derek Pua, Danielle Dybbro, & Alistair Rogers, *Unit 731: The Forgotten Auschwitz*. Pacific Atrocities Education, 2018.

Stacey Anne Baterina Salinas & Klytie Xu, *Philippines' Resistance: The Last Allied Stronghold in the Pacific*. Pacific Atrocities Education, 2017.

Rijuta Vallishayee and Tessa Delgo. *Rice and Revolution: The Great Famine of Vietnam during World War II, 1944-1945*. Pacific Atrocities Education, 2021.

Works Cited

Books

Arrizon, Alicia. *Queering Mestizaje: Transculturation and Performance*. Ann Arbor: University of Michigan Press, 2009.

Atwood, Kathryn J. *Women Heroes of World War II: The Pacific Theater, 15 Stories of Resistance, Rescue, Sabotage, and Survival*. Chicago: Chicago Review Press Incorporated, 2017.

Bayor, Ronald H. *Multicultural America: An Encyclopedia of the Newest Americans*. Santa Barbara: ABC-CLIO LLC., 2011.

Bennett, Tom. *World War II Wrecks of the Philippines: WWII Shipwrecks of the Philippines*. Philippines: Happy Fish Publications, 2010.

Boyer, Robert H. *Sundays in Manila*. Quezon City: The University of the Philippines Press, 2010.

Buell, Thomas B., John H. Bradley, and Jack W. Dice, *The Second World War: Asia and the Pacific*. Singapore: Square One Publishers, 2002.

Dahl, Erik J. *Intelligence and Surprise Attack: Failure and Success from Pearl Harbor to 9/11 and Beyond*. Georgetown University Press, 2013.

Del Castillo y Tuazon, Antonio. *Princess Urduja, Queen of the Orient Seas: Before and After her Time in the*

Political Orbit of the Shri-vi-ja-ya and the Madjapahit Maritime Empire: a Pre-Hispanic History of the Philippines. University of Michigan, 1998.

Chun, Clayton. *The Fall of the Philippines, 1941-1942*. Osprey Publishing, 2012.

Cuizon, Erma M. *Twilight in Misamis: Josefa Borromeo Capistrano's Guerrilla Days*. Cebu City: University of San Carlos Press, 2014.

Cruz, Denise. *Transpacific Femininities: The Making of the Modern Filipina*. Durham & London: Duke University Press, 2012.

Duka, Cecilio D. *Struggle for Freedom*. Manila: Rex Publishing, 2008.

Greenberger, Robert. *Snapshots in History: The Bataan Death March: World War II in the Pacific*. Mankato: Compass Point Books, 2009.

Henson, Maria Rosa. *Comfort Woman: A Filipina's Story of Prostitution and Slavery Under the Japanese Military*. London: Rowman & Littlefield, 2017.

Hing, Bill Ong. *Making and Remaking Asian America Through Immigration Policy: 1850-1990*. Stanford: Stanford University Press, 1993.

Ikehata, Setsuho & Ricardo Trota Jose. *The Philippines Under Japan: Occupation Policy and Reaction*. University of Hawaii Press, 1999.

Ingham, Travis. *Rendezvous By Submarine: The Story of Charles Parsons and the Guerrilla-Soldiers in the Philippines*. Los Angeles: The Bowsprit Press, 2018.

Ishida, Miki Y. *Toward Peace: War Responsibility, Postwar Compensation, and Peace Movements and Education in Japan*. New York: iUniverse, Inc., 2005.

Jacob, Frank. *Japanese War Crimes During World War II: Atrocity and Psychology of Collective Violence*. Santa Barbara: Frank Jacob, 2018.

Kaminski, Theresa. *Angels of the Underground: The American Women Who Resisted the Japanese in World War II*. New York: Oxford University Press, 2016.

Kaminski, Theresa. *Prisoners in Paradise: American Women in the Wartime South Pacific*. University Press of Kansas, 2000.

Keats, John. *They Fought Alone: A True Story of an American Hero*. Echo Point Books and Media, 2015.

Kim, Eileen Yujoo. *Korean Comfort Women: Political and Personal History Intertwined*. Berkeley: University of California Press, 1997.

Lansdale, Edward Geary. *In the Midst of Wars: An American's Mission to Southeast Asia*. New York: Fordham University Press, 1991.

Lanzona, Vina A. *Amazons of the Huk Rebellion: Gender, Sex, and Revolution in the Philippines*. Madison: University of Wisconsin Press, 2009.

Leary, William M. ed., *We Shall Return!: MacArthur's Commanders and the Defeat of Japan, 1942-1945*. Lexington: The University of Kentucky Press, 1988.

Lee, Ernesto. *World War II Philippines: A Boy's Tale of Survival*. Xlibris Corporation, 2010.

Li, Peter ed. *Japanese War Crimes*. New Brunswick: Routledge, 2017.

Maceda, Teresita Gimenez. *Bride of War: My Mother's World War II Memories*. Mandaluyong City: Anvil Publishing, 2011.

Maga, Timothy P. *Judgement at Tokyo: The Japanese War Crimes Trials*. Lexington: University of Press of Kentucky, 2001.

Marinari, Maddalena, Madeline Hsu, Maria Cristina Garcia ed. *A Nation of Immigrants Reconsidered: US Society in an Age of Restriction, 1924-1965*. University of Illinois Press, 2018.

Masato Kimura, Tosh Minohara ed. *Tumultuous Decade: Empire, Society, and Diplomacy in 1930s Japan*. Toronto: University of Toronto Press, 2013.

Masuda, Hiroshi. *MacArthur in Asia: The General and His Staff in the Philippines, Japan, and Korea*. London: Cornell University Press, 2009.

McCoy, Alfred W. *Policing America's Empire: The United States, The Philippines, and the Rise of the Surveillance State*. Madison: University of Wisconsin Press, 2009.

Mills, Scott. *Stranded in the Philippines: Professor Bell's Private War Against the Japanese*. Annapolis: Naval Institute Press, 2009.

Molnar, Nicholas Trajano. *American Mestizos, The Philippines, and the Malleability of Race:1898-1961*. University of Missouri Press, 2017.

Montgomery, Ben. *Leper Spy: The Story of an Unlikely Hero of World War II*. Illinois: Chicago Review Press Incorporated, 2017.

Morton, Louis. *The War in the Pacific: Strategy and Command, the First Two Years.* Washington D.C.: Center of Military History United States Army, 2000.

Morton, Louis. *United States Army in World War II: The War in the Pacific—Fall of the Philippines.* Washington, DC: Office of the Chief of Military History, Department of the Army, 1953.

Murphy, Kevin C. *Inside the Bataan Death March: Defeat, Travail and Memory.* Jefferson: McFarland, 2014.

Nadal, Kevin L. *Filipino American Psychology: A Handbook of Theory, Research, and Clinical Practice.* Bloomington: Authorhouse, 2009.

Nalty, Bernard C., ed. *War in the Pacific: Pearl Harbor to Tokyo Bay, the Story of the Bitter Struggle in the Pacific Theater of World War II.* Norman: University of Oklahoma Press, 1999.

National Centennial Commission, *Sulong Pilipina! Sulong Pilipinas!: A Compilation of Filipino Women Centennial Awardees.* National Centennial Commission, Women Sector, 1999.

Norman, Elizabeth M. *We Band of Angels: The Untold Story of the American Women Trapped on Bataan.* New York: Random House Trade Paperback, 2013.

Nuval, Leonardo Q. *Remember Them Kindly: Some Filipinos During World War II.* Claretian Publications, 1996.

Panicello, Joseph Francis. *A Slow Moving Target: The LST of World War II.* Joseph Francis Panicello, 2001.

Panlilio, Yay. *The Crucible: An Autobiography by Colonel Yay, Filipina American Guerrilla*. New Brunswick: Rutgers University Press, 1950.

Perry, Mark. *The Most Dangerous Man in America: The Making of Douglas MacArthur*. New York: Basic Books, 2014.

Polette, Nancy. *P.O.W. Angel on Call: The True Story of an American Guerrilla Nurse in the Philippines During World War II*. Blessinks, 2013.

Poole, Peter A. *Politics and Society in Southeast Asia*. North Carolina: McFarland & Company, 2009.

Rodao, Florentine and Felice Noelle Rodriguez ed. *The Philippine Revolution of 1896: Ordinary Lives in Extraordinary Times*. Manila: Ateneo de Manila University Press, 2001.

Sinclair II, Major Peter T. *Men of Destiny: The American and Filipino Guerrillas During the Japanese Occupation of the Philippines*. Pickle Partners Publishing, 2015.

Sohoni, Deenesh & Amin Vafa. "The Fight to Be American: Military Naturalization, and Asian Citizenship." *Asian American Law Journal*. Vol. 17 Article 4 (January 2010): 119-151.

Spencer, Louise Reid. *Guerrilla Wife*. Pickle Partners Publishing, 2017.

Stetz, Margaret D. & Bonnie B. C. Oh ed. *Legacies of the Comfort Women of World War II*. New York: Routledge, 2015.

Tanaka, Toshiyuki. *Hidden Horrors: Japanese War Crimes in World War II*. Westview Press, 1996.

Triplet, William S. *In the Philippines and Okinawa: A Memoir, 1945-1948.* Columbia: University of Missouri Press, 2001.

Tsai, Shih-Shan Henry. *Maritime Taiwan: Historical Encounters with the East and the West.* Taylor and Francis, 2014.

Waines, Davis. *The Odyssey of Ibn Battuta: Uncommon Tales of a Medieval Adventurer.* New York: I.B. Tauris & Co, 2010.

Walker, D.J. *Spanish Women and the Colonial Wars.* Baton Rouge: Louisiana State University Press, May 2008.

Willbanks, James H., ed. *Generals of the Army: Marshall, MacArthur, Eisenhower, Arnold, Bradley.* Lexington: University of Kentucky Press, 2013.

Wynn, Neil A. *Historical Dictionary from the Great War to the Great Depression.* Lanham: Scarecrow Press, 2014.

Yoshiaki, Yoshimi. *Comfort Women: Sexual Slavery in the Japanese Military During World War II.* New York: Columbia University Press, 1995.

Journal Articles

Lanzona, Vina A. "Capturing the Huk Amazons: Representing Women Warriors in the Philippines, 1940s-1950s." *South East Asia Research*, Vol. 17 No. 2 (July 2009): 133-174.

Sergeant Karl Ritt. "Filipino Nurses on Bataan." *American Journal of Nursing*, Vol. 45 No. 5 (May 1945): 346-347.

Government Sources

The U.S. National Archives and Records Administration. "Military Records: Guerrilla Units." *The Philippine Archives Collection*. https://www.archives.gov/research/military/ww2/philippine/guerrilla-list-1.html.

The U.S. National Archives and Records Administration. "Guerrilla Unit Recognition Files, 1941-1948." *The Philippine Archives Collection*. https://catalog.archives.gov/id/1257644.

U.S. Department of Veterans Affairs. WWII Filipino Veterans Equity Compensation (FVEC) Fund." *Center for Minority Veterans*. Last modified April 11th, 2018. https://www.va.gov/centerforminorityveterans/fvec.asp.

Theses

Larry S. Schmidt. *American Involvement in the Filipino Resistance Movement on Mindanao During the Japanese Occupation, 1942-1945, Master of Military Art and Science Thesis*. U.S. Army Command and General Staff College, 1982.

News & Internet Resources

ABS-CBN News Correspondent. "Last Hukbalahap Commander Dies, Age 92." *ABS-CBN.com*. Last mo-

Works Cited

dified July 3, 2015. Last accessed August 17th, 2018. http://news.abs-cbn.com/nation/regions/07/02/15/last-hukbalahap-commander-dies-age-92.

Arcellaz, Princess Clea. "San Simon Pays Tribute to Kumander Guerrero." *Sun Star Philippines*. Last modified July 5th, 2015. Last accessed August 17th, 2018. https://www.sunstar.com.ph/article/18277/.

Bartolome, Jessica. "Kumander Guerrero will Live On: Remembering Simeona Tapang." last modified July 7th, 2015. Last accessed August 17th, 2018, http://www.gmanetwork.com/news/lifestyle/content/517646/kumander-guerrero-will-live-on-remembering-simeona-tapang/story/.

Caballes, "10 Kickass Pilipina Warriors that You Probably Never Heard of," *Pinoy Culture.com: Your Source for Everything Pilipino*, last modified August 28th, 2014, last accessed August 23rd, 2018, http://pinoy-culture.com/10-kickass-pilipina-warriors-in-history-that-you-probably-never-heard-of/.

Cabico, Gaea Katreena. "Gabriela Solons Seek Probe into Removal of Comfort Woman Statue." *PhilStar News*, last modified May 10th, 2018. Last accessed December 28th, 2018. https://www.philstar.com/headlines/2018/05/10/1813942/gabriela-solons-seek-probe-removal-comfort-woman-statue.

Celdran, Beatrice. "I Am… Woman: Historic Filipinas." *Philippine Tatler*. Last modified August 7th, 2014. Last accessed August 23rd, 2018, https://ph.asiatatler.com/life/i-am-woman.

Chua, Xiao. "'Lioness of PHL guerilla spies' Maggie Leones To Be Buried With Full Honors." *GMA News Online*. Last modified June 11th, 2016. Last accessed December 27th, 2018. https://www.gmanetwork.com/news/lifestyle/content/573214/lioness-of-phl-guerilla-spies-maggie-leones-to-be-buried-with-full-honors/story/.

Chua, Xiao. "JOSEFA LLANES ESCODA AT ANG MGA PASAWAY NA BABAE NOONG DIGMAAN." *It's Xiao Time!* Last modified January 31st, 2013. Last accessed August 17th, 2018. https://xiaochua.net/2013/01/31/xiaotime-31-january-2013-josefa-llanes-escoda-at-ang-mga-pasaway-na-babae-noong-digmaan/.

Dietz, Lorna. "The Story of a Rare and Great Hero." *Scribd*. Last modified December 2011. Last accessed August 17th, 2018. https://www.scribd.com/document/75503075/Lourdes-Castro-1926-2011-The-Story-of-a-Rare-and-Great-Hero.

Estrella, Cicero A. "Filipinos had to Fight for the Right to Serve their Adopted Home." *San Francisco Gate*. Last modified May 5th, 2005, last accessed November 13th, 2021. https://www.sfgate.com/entertainment/article/Filipinos-had-to-fight-for-right-to-serve-their-2632699.php.

FilipiKnow.net. "The 10 Most Incredible Filipina Warriors of World War II." *FilipiKnow*. Last modified 2018, last accessed December 17th, 2018. https://filipiknow.net/filipina-heroes-of-wwii/#2_Elena_Poblete.

Works Cited

GMA News. "Last Living Huk Commander Passes Away a Day Before Her 93rd Birthday." *GMA News Online*. Last modified July 2, 2015. Last accessed December 18th, 2018. https://www.gmanetwork.com/news/lifestyle/content/514518/last-living-huk-commander-passes-away-a-day-before-93rd-birthday/story/.

Guillermo, Emil. "Magdalena Leones, Filipina World War II Silver Star Recipient Who Aided MacArthur, Dies in California." Last modified July 5th, 2016. Last accessed August 17th, 2018. https://www.nbcnews.com/news/asian-america/magdalena-leones-filipina-wwii-silver-star-recepient-who-aided-macarthur-n603566.

IMDB. "American Guerrilla in the Philippines." *IMDB.com*. https://www.imdb.com/title/tt0042195.

Jayme, Tessie. "Red Cross in Manila." *Black Clouds in Manila*. Last modified March 1st, 2014. Last Accessed August 17th, 2018. http://blackcloudsinmanila.com/Home.php.

Koa, Fannie Tan. "The Wha Chi Guerrillas." *The Philippine Star*. Last Modified May 24, 2015. Last accessed November 14, 2021. https://www.pressreader.com/philippines/the-philippine-star/20150524/283536564341187.

De Leon, Dwight. "WWII Filipina Spy Dies at 95." *Rappler News, Philippines*. Last modified June 24th, 2016. Last accessed August 17th, 2018. https://www.rappler.com/move-ph/137362-world-war-filipina-spy-magdalena-leones.

Maceda, Marichu. "Carmen Rosales: The Genuine Superstar." *PhilStar Global*. Last modified March 6th, 2005. Last accessed December 27th, 2018. https://www.philstar.com/entertainment/2005/03/06/269261/carmen-rosales-genuine-superstar.

Orejas, Tonette. "Pension Elusive for Aeta Guerrillas." *Inquirer.Net*. Last modified March 2nd, 2014. Last accessed December 28th, 2018. https://newsinfo.inquirer.net/769917/pension-elusive-for-aeta-guerrillas.

Orejas, Tonette. "Liwayway: Warrior Who Wore Lipstick in Gun Battles." *Inquirer.Net Central Luzon*. Last modified May 17th, 2014. Last accessed August 17th, 2018. https://newsinfo.inquirer.net/602758/liwayway-warrior-who-wore-lipstick-in-gun-battles.

Osaki, Tomohiro. "Abe Rejects Seoul's New Call for Apology On 'Comfort Women' Issue." *Japan Times*. Last modified January 12th, 2018. Last accessed December 21st, 2018. https://www.japantimes.co.jp/news/2018/01/12/national/politics-diplomacy/abe-rejects-kangs-new-apology-call-comfort-women-issue/.

Palafox, Quennie Ann J. "Lest We Forget our Unsung Founding Mothers." *Inquirer.Net*. Last modified June 12th, 2011. Accessed August 17th, 2018. http://newsinfo.inquirer.net/14134/lest-we-forget-our-unsung-founding-mothers.

Pre-Medical Society of the Ateneo. "Filipina Angels of Bataan." *The Pre-Medical Society of the Ateneo*. Last modified April 9th, 2015. Last accessed December 27th, 2018.

Works Cited

Rare Historical Photos. "Captain Nieves Fernandez Shows to an American Soldier how She Used her Long Knife to Silently Kill Japanese Soldiers During Occupation, 1944." *RareHistoricalPhotos.com*. Last modified June 21st, 2014. Last accessed August 17th, 2018. https://rarehistoricalphotos.com/captain-nieves-fernandez-1944/.

Richardson, Jim. "Celia Mariano Pomeroy: Communist Revolutionary Who Went on to Teach in London Primary Schools." *Independent Minds*. Last modified October 22, 2009, last accessed December 18th, 2018. https://www.independent.co.uk/news/obituaries/celia-mariano-pomeroy-communist-revolutionary-who-went-on-to-teach-in-london-primary-schools-1806786.html.

Sellers, Michael. "Captain Nieves Fernandez—WWII Guerrilla Leader in Leyte, Philippines." *Michael Sellers.com*. Last modified February 11th, 2017. Last accessed August 15th, 2018. http://www.michaelsellers.com/blog/2017/02/11/looking-for-info-on-captain-nieves-fernandez-wwii-guerrilla-leader-in-leyte-philippines/.

Snafu, Doc. "(USAFFE) (Far East) Guerrilla Movement, Philippines, 1942-1945." *EUCMH Exposition Blog*. Last modified July 17th, 2015. Last accessed August 15th, 2018. https://www.eucmh.com/2015/07/17/usaffe-far-east-guerrilla-movement-philippines-1942-1945/.

Tantingco, Robby. "Why Women Rule Pampanga." *Positively Filipino: Your Window on the Filipino Diaspora*.

Last modified March 10th, 2015. Last accessed August 17th, 2018. http://www.positivelyfilipino.com/magazine/why-women-rule-pampanga.

Templo, Mike. "Claiming Veterans' Benefits Under Obama's Stimulus Package-Atty. Mike Templo." Last modified February 28th, 2009. Last accessed August 20th, 2018. http://news.abs-cbn.com/views-and-analysis/02/27/09/claiming-veterans-benefits-under-obamas-stimulus-package-atty-mike-templ.

Unknown Author. "School Ma'am Led Guerrillas On Leyte." *Lewiston Daily Sun*, October 26th, 1944. Last accessed August 15th, 2018. http://www.michaeldsellers.com/blog/2017/02/11/looking-for-info-on-captain-nieves-fernandez-wwii-guerrilla-leader-in-leyte-philippines/.

Video 48. "Carmen Rosales." *Video 48: A Virtual Online Library and Archive On Philippine Cinema*. Last modified April 30th 2008. Last accessed December 27th, 2018. http://video48.blogspot.com/search?q=-Carmen+Rosales.

Video 48, "THE FIFTIES # 618: PANCHO MAGALONA AND ROSA ROSAL IN LAMBERTO V. AVELLANA'S "CRY FREEDOM" (1959)," *Video48: A Virtual Online Library and Archive of Philippine Cinema*, last modified April 22nd, 2014, last accessed December 27th, 2018. http://video48.blogspot.com/2014/04/the-fifties-618-pancho-magalona-and.html.

Watawat.net. "The Wha-Chi and Other Guerrilla Groups and Units." *Watawat: Flags and Symbols of the Pearl of the Orient Seas*, last modified 2017. Last accessed December 17th, 2018. http://www.watawat.net/the-wha-chi--and-other-guerrilla-groups-and-units.html.

Welteke, Karl. "Corregidor-Then and Now: 503rd PRCT Heritage Battalion, The Fall of the Philippines, Battle of Manila." *Corregidorproboards.com*, last modified August 3rd, 2015. Last accessed December 22nd, 2018. http://corregidor.proboards.com/thread/1848/general-wainwright.

Yoder, Robert L. "Philippine Heroines of the Revolution: Maria Clara They Were Not." *Austrian-Philippine*. Last modified September 1st, 1999. Last accessed August 17th, 2018. https://www.univie.ac.at/ksa/apsis/aufi/wstat/heroine.htm.

Archives, Oral Histories, & Personal Collections

Aremas, Sherry. World War II Philippine Guerrilla, Salinas *Manang* Pre-1965 Generation. Interviewed by Stacey Salinas. April 2018.

Aremas, Susan. Bridge Generation Filipina American, Primary School Teacher, Daughter of the *Manong* Generation. Interviewed by Stacey Salinas. January-April 2018.

Congressional Record. *United States of America: Congressional Record: Proceedings and Debates of the 111th Congress, First Session*. Washington: United States Government Printing Office, 2009.

Danny Dolor. "Carmen Rosales as Guerilyera." Last modified June 14th, 2014. Last accessed December 27th, 2018. https://www.pressreader.com/philippines/the-philippine-star/20150614/282402693010462.

Dawang, Bienvenida Pedraza. World War II, Sacramento and Stockton, *Manang* Pre-1965 Generation. Interviewed by Stacey Salinas, 2019.

Dec, Billy. "Honoring Filipino WWII Veterans This Filipino American History Month." *The White House: President Barack Obama.* Last Modified October 3rd, 2016. Last accessed December 24th, 2018. https://obamawhitehouse.archives.gov/blog/2016/10/03/honoring-filipino-wwii-veterans-filipino-american-history-month.

Garcia, Almira Albarico. World War II, Los Angeles Manila Town, *Manang* Pre-1965 Generation. Interviewed by Stacey Salinas, 2019.

The Philippines Mail. Microfilm. John Steinbeck Public Library, Salinas, California. Photographs. Aremas Family Personal Collection. Salinas, California.

Magallanes, Ofelia. World War II, Luzon, Cavite City. Interviewed by Abby Gayle Principe, 2018.

Magallanes, Ofelia. "Ofelia After the War." Photograph. 1940s. Magallanes-Principe Family Collection.

Orpilla, Ofelia Galvez. World War II Philippine Guerrilla, Vallejo *Manang* pre-1965 Generation. Interviewed by Stacey Salinas, 2020.

Poblete, Lourdes. World War II Guerrilla, Filipina American Medical Worker. Interviewed by Stacey Salinas. June 2017.

Works Cited

The U.S. National Archives and Records Administration. "Military Records: Guerrilla Units." *The Philippine Archives Collection*. https://www.archives.gov/research/military/ww2/philippine/guerrilla-list-1.html.

The U.S. National Archives and Records Administration. "Guerrilla Unit Recognition Files, 1941-1948." *The Philippine Archives Collection*. https://catalog.archives.gov/id/1257644.

The U.S. National Archives and Records Administration. "Department of Defense. Far East Command. Philippines Command. Guerrilla Affairs Division. 8/1/1948-10/14/1949." Series: Records Relating to the U.S. Army Recognition Program of Philippine Guerrillas, ca. 1949—ca. 1949 Record Group 554: Records of General Headquarters, Far East Command, Supreme Commander Allied Powers, and United Nations Command, 1945-1960, https://catalog.archives.gov/id/6921767.

U.S. Citizenship and Immigration Services. "USCIS to Implement Filipino World War II Veterans Parole Program. *USCIS*. Last modified May 9th, 2016. Last accessed December 24th, 2018. https://www.uscis.gov/news/news-releases/uscis-implement-filipino-world-war-ii-veterans-parole-program.

Westpoint. "Guerrillas in the Philippines." *West-Point.org*. http://www.west-point.org/family/japanese-pow/Guerrillas/Guerrillas-Main.htm.

Films

Magalona, Pancho & Rosa Rosal. *Cry Freedom*. Directed by Lamberto V. Avellana. Parallel Film Distribution, Inc., Metro Manila, 1959.

Power, Tyrone & Micheline Presle. *American Guerrilla in the Philippines* 1950. Directed by Fritz Lang. 20th Century Fox, 1950.

De La Rosa, Rogelio & Norma Blancaflor. *Victory Joe*. Directed by Manuel Silos. LVN Pictures, Metro Manila, 1946.

Rosales, Carmen & Jaime De La Rosa. *Batalyon XIII*. Directed by Manuel Silos. LVN Pictures, Metro Manila, 1949.

Rosales, Carmen & Tita Dura. *Guerilyera*. Directed by Octavio Silos. Sampaguita Pictures, 1946.

Title Page Photograph

"Anti-worlds," *Tumblr*, https://bag-of-dirt.tumblr.com/post/70453965715/a-young-filipino-resistance-fighter-poses-with-a.

Made in the USA
Monee, IL
30 August 2024